CIMA Exam Practice Kit

C000089385

Fundamentals of Business Mathematics

CIMA Exam Practice Kit

CIMA
PUBLISHING

Fundamentals of Business Mathematics

CIMA Certificate in Business Accounting

Walter Allan and Jo Avis

ELSEVIER   Amsterdam • Boston • Heidelberg • London • New York • Oxford
Paris • San Diego • San Francisco • Singapore • Sydney • Tokyo

CIMA Publishing is an imprint of Elsevier
Linacre House, Jordan Hill, Oxford OX2 8DP, UK
30 Corporate Drive, Suite 400, Burlington, MA 01803, USA

First edition 2008

Copyright © 2008, Elsevier Ltd. All rights reserved

No part of this publication may be reproduced, stored in a retrieval system
or transmitted in any form or by any means electronic, mechanical, photocopying,
recording or otherwise without the prior written permission of the publisher

Permissions may be sought directly from Elsevier's Science & Technology Rights
Department in Oxford, UK: phone: (+44) (0) 1865 843830; fax: (+44) (0) 1865 853333;
e-mail: permissions@elsevier.com. Alternatively you can submit your request online by
visiting the Elsevier web site at http://elsevier.com/locate/permissions, and selecting
Obtaining permission to use Elsevier material

Notice
No responsibility is assumed by the publisher for any injury and/or damage to persons
or property as a matter of products liability, negligence or otherwise, or from any use
or operation of any methods, products, instructions or ideas contained in the material
herein. Because of rapid advances in the medical sciences, in particular, independent
verification of diagnoses and drug dosages should be made

British Library Cataloguing in Publication Data
A catalogue record for this book is available from the British Library

978 0 7506 8718 8

For information on all CIMA Publishing Publications
visit our web site at www.cimapublishing.com

Printed and bound in Hungary

08 09 10 11 12   10 9 8 7 6 5 4 3 2 1

Working together to grow
libraries in developing countries

www.elsevier.com | www.bookaid.org | www.sabre.org

ELSEVIER   BOOK AID
             International   Sabre Foundation

Contents

About the Author

Walter Allan is a graduate of Heriot-Watt University where he specialized in Mathematical Economics and probability theory. He has extensive lecturing experience in both the public and private sectors. He is responsible for the teaching of economics at Cass Business School, London and the Actuarial Science Degree.

Syllabus Guidance, Learning Objectives and Verbs

A The Certificate in Business Accounting

The Certificate introduces you to management accounting and gives you the basics of accounting and business. There are five subject areas, which are all tested by computer-based assessment (CBA). The five papers are:

- Fundamentals of Management Accounting
- Fundamentals of Financial Accounting
- Fundamentals of Business Mathematics
- Fundamentals of Business Economics
- Fundamentals of Ethics, Corporate Governance and Business Law

The Certificate is both a qualification in its own right and an entry route to the next stage in CIMA's examination structure.

The examination structure after the Certificate comprises:

- Managerial Level
- Strategic Level
- Test of Professional Competence (an exam based on a case study).

B Aims of the syllabus

The aims of the syllabus are:

- to provide for the Institute, together with the practical experience requirements, an adequate basis for assuring society that those admitted to membership are competent to act as management accountants for entities, whether in manufacturing, commercial or service organisations, in the public or private sectors of the economy;
- to enable the Institute to examine whether prospective members have an adequate knowledge, understanding and mastery of the stated body of knowledge and skills;
- to complement the Institute's practical experience and skills development requirements.

C Study weightings

A percentage weighting is shown against each topic in the syllabus. This is intended as a guide to the proportion of study time each topic requires.

All topics in the syllabus must be studied, since any single examination question may examine more than one topic, or carry a higher proportion of marks than the percentage study time suggested.

The weightings *do not* specify the number of marks that will be allocated to topics in the examination.

D Learning outcomes

Each topic within the syllabus contains a list of learning outcomes, which should be read in conjunction with the knowledge content for the syllabus. A learning outcome has two main purposes:

1   to define the skill or ability that a well-prepared candidate should be able to exhibit in the examination;
2   to demonstrate the approach likely to be taken by examiners in examination questions.

The learning outcomes are part of a hierarchy of learning objectives. The verbs used at the beginning of each learning outcome relate to a specific learning objective, for example, evaluate alternative approaches to budgeting.

The verb 'evaluate' indicates a high level learning objective. As learning objectives are hierarchical, it is expected that at this level, students will have knowledge of different budgeting systems and methodologies and be able to apply them.

A list of the learning objectives and the verbs that appear in the syllabus learning outcomes and examinations, follows:

Learning objectives	*Verbs used*	*Definition*
1 Knowledge		
What you are expected to know	List	Make a list of
	State	Express, fully or clearly, the details of/facts of
	Define	Give the exact meaning of
2 Comprehension		
What you are expected to understand	Describe	Communicate the key features of
	Distinguish	Highlight the differences between
	Explain	Make clear or intelligible/State the meaning of
	Identify	Recognise, establish or select after consideration
	Illustrate	Use an example to describe or explain something

3 Application

How you are expected to apply your knowledge	Apply	To put to practical use
	Calculate/ compute	To ascertain or reckon mathematically
	Demonstrate	To prove with certainty or to exhibit by practical means
	Prepare	To make or get ready for use
	Reconcile	To make or prove consistent/ compatible
	Solve	Find an answer to
	Tabulate	Arrange in a table

4 Analysis

How you are expected to analyse the detail of what you have learned	Analyse	Examine in detail the structure of
	Categorise	Place into a defined class or division
	Compare and contrast	Show the similarities and/or differences between
	Construct	To build up or compile
	Discuss	To examine in detail by argument
	Interpret	To translate into intelligible or familiar terms
	Produce	To create or bring into existence

5 Evaluation

How you are expected to use your learning to evaluate, make decisions or recommendations	Advise	To counsel, inform or notify
	Evaluate	To appraise or assess the value of
	Recommend	To advise on a course of action

Computer-based assessment

CIMA has introduced computer-based assessment (CBA) for all subjects at Certificate level. The website says

> Objective questions are used. The most common type is 'multiple choice', where you have to choose the correct answer from a list of possible answers, but there are a variety of other objective question types that can be used within the system. These include true/false questions, matching pairs of text and graphic, sequencing and ranking, labelling diagrams and single and multiple numeric entry.

> Candidates answer the questions by either pointing and clicking the mouse, moving objects around the screen, typing numbers, or a combination of these responses. Try the online demo at [http://www.cimaglobal.com] to get a feel for how the technology will work.

> The CBA system can ensure that a wide range of the syllabus is assessed, as a pre-determined number of questions from each syllabus area (dependent upon the syllabus weighting for that particular area) are selected in each assessment.

In every chapter of the Learning system, we introduced these types of questions. There will be scenario type questions in the CBA but they will rarely have more than three sub-questions. In all such cases examiners will ensure that the answer to one part does not hinge upon a prior answer.

There are two types of questions which were previously involved in objective testing in paper-based exams and which are not at present possible in a CBA. The actual drawing of graphs and charts is not yet possible. Equally there will be no questions calling for – comments to be written by students. Charts and interpretations remain on many syllabi and will be examined at Certificate level but using other methods.

For further CBA practice, CIMA Publishing is producing CIMA e-success CD-ROMs for all Certificate level subjects. These products are available at www.cimapublishing.com.

Fundamentals of Business Mathematics

Syllabus outline

The syllabus comprises:

Topic and study weighting

A	Basic Mathematics	15%
B	Probability	15%
C	Summarising and Analysing Data	15%
D	Interrelationship between Variables	15%
E	Forecasting	15%
F	Financial Mathematics	15%
G	Spreadsheets	10%

Learning aims

This syllabus aims to test the student's ability to:

- demonstrate the use of basic mathematics, including formulae and ratios;
- identify reasonableness in the calculation of answers;
- demonstrate the use of probability where risk and uncertainty exist;
- apply techniques for summarising and analysing data;
- calculate correlation coefficients for bivariate data and apply the technique of simple regression analysis;
- demonstrate techniques used for forecasting;
- apply financial mathematical techniques;
- apply spreadsheets to facilitate the presentation of data, analysis of univariate and bivariate data and use of formulae.

Assessment strategy

There will be a computer-based assessment of 2 hours duration, comprising 45 compulsory questions, each with one or more parts.
A variety of objective test question styles and types will be used within the assessment.

Learning outcomes and indicative syllabus content

A Basic Mathematics – 15%

Learning outcomes

On completion of their studies students should be able to:

- demonstrate the order of operations in formulae, including brackets, powers and roots;
- calculate percentages and proportions;
- calculate answers to an appropriate number of decimal places or significant figures;
- solve simple equations, including two variable simultaneous equations and quadratic equations;
- prepare graphs of linear and quadratic equations.

Indicative syllabus content

- Use of formulae, including negative powers as in the formula for the learning curve.
- Percentages and ratios.
- Rounding of numbers.
- Basic algebraic techniques and solution of equations, including simultaneous equations and quadratic equations.
- Manipulation of inequalities.

B Probability – 15%

Learning outcomes

On completion of their studies students should be able to:

- calculate a simple probability;
- demonstrate the addition and multiplication rules of probability;
- calculate a simple conditional probability;
- calculate an expected value;
- demonstrate the use of expected value tables in decision-making;
- explain the limitations of expected values;
- explain the concepts of risk and uncertainty.

Indicative syllabus content

- The relationship between probability, proportion and per cent.
- Addition and multiplication rules in probability theory.
- Venn diagrams.
- Expected values and expected value tables.
- Risk and uncertainty.

C Summarising and Analysing Data – 15%

Learning outcomes

On completion of their studies students should be able to:

- explain the difference between data and information;
- identify the characteristics of good information;
- tabulate data and prepare histograms;

- calculate for both ungrouped and grouped data: arithmetic mean, median, mode, range, variance, standard deviation and coefficient of variation;
- explain the concept of a frequency distribution;
- prepare graphs/diagrams of normal distribution, explain its properties and use tables of normal distribution;
- apply the Pareto distribution and the '80:20 rule'.
- explain how and why indices are used;
- calculate indices using either base or current weights;
- apply indices to deflate a series.

Indicative syllabus content

- Data and information.
- Tabulation of data.
- Graphs and diagrams: scatter diagrams, histograms, bar charts and gives.
- Summary measures of central tendency and dispersion for both grouped and ungrouped data.
- Frequency distributions.
- Normal distribution, the Pareto distribution and the '80:20 rule'.
- Index numbers.

D   Interrelationship between Variables – 15%

Learning outcomes

On completion of their studies students should be able to:

- prepare a scatter diagram;
- calculate the correlation coefficient and the coefficient of determination between two variables;
- calculate the regression equation between two variables;
- apply the regression equation to predict the dependent variable, given a value of the independent variable.

Indicative syllabus content

- Scatter diagrams and the correlation coefficient.
- Simple linear regression.

E   Forecasting – 15%

Learning outcomes

On completion of their studies students should be able to:

- prepare a time series graph;
- identify trends and patterns using an appropriate moving average;
- identify the components of a time series model;
- prepare a trend equation using either graphical means or regression analysis;
- calculate seasonal factors for both additive and multiplicative models and explain when each is appropriate;
- calculate predicated values, given a time series model;
- identify the limitations of forecasting models.

Indicative syllabus content

- Time series analysis – graphical analysis.
- Trends in time series – graphs, moving averages and linear regression.
- Seasonal variations using both additive and multiplicative models.
- Forecasting and its limitations.

F   Financial Mathematics – 15%

Learning outcomes

On completion of their studies students should be able to:

- calculate future values of an investment using both simple and compound interest;
- calculate an annual percentage rate of interest given a monthly or quarterly rate;
- calculate the present value of a future cash sum using formula and CIMA Tables;
- calculate the present value of an annuity and a perpetuity using formula and CIMA Tables;
- calculate loan/mortgage repayments and the value of the loan/mortgage outstanding;
- calculate the future value of regular savings and/or the regular investment needed to generate a required future sum using the formula for the sum of a geometric progression;
- calculate the net present value (NPV) and internal rate of return (IRR) of a project and explain whether and why it should be accepted.

Indicative syllabus content

- Simple and compound interest.
- Annuities and perpetuities.
- Loans and mortgages.
- Sinking funds and savings funds.
- Discounting to find NPV and IRR, and interpretation of NPV and IRR.

G   Spreadsheets – 10%

Learning outcomes

On completion of their studies students should be able to:

- explain the features and functions of spreadsheet software;
- explain the use and limitations of spreadsheet software in business;
- apply spreadsheet software to the normal work of a Chartered Management Accountant.

Indicative syllabus content

- Features and functions of commonly used spreadsheet software: workbook, worksheet, rows, columns, cells, data, text, formulae, formatting, printing, graphics and macros. Note: Knowledge of Microsoft Excel type spreadsheet vocabulary/formulae syntax is required. Formulae tested will be that which is constructed by users rather than pre-programmed formulae.
- Advantages and disadvantages of spreadsheet software, when compared to manual analysis and other types of software application packages.
- Use of spreadsheet software in the day-to-day work of the Chartered Management Accountant: budgeting, forecasting, reporting performance, variance analysis, 'what–if–?' analysis, discounted cashflow calculations.

Examination Techniques

Computer-based examinations

10 Golden rules

1   Make sure you are familiar with software before you start the exam. You cannot speak to invigilator once you have started.
2   These exam practice kits give you plenty of exam style questions to practice.
3   Attempt all questions, there is no negative marking.
4   Double check your answer before you put in final alternative.
5   On multiple choice questions, there is only one correct answer.
6   Not all questions will be MCQs – you may have to fill in missing words or figures.
7   Identify the easy questions first, get some points on the board to build up your confidence.
8   Try and allow five minutes at the end to check your answers and make any corrections.
9   If you don't know the answer, try process of elimination. Sadly there is no phone a friend!!
10 Take scrap paper, pen and calculator with you. Work out answer on paper first if it is easier for you.

Mathematical tables

Probability

$A ✤ B = A$ or B. $A ∩ B = A$ and B (overlap).
$P(B|A)$ = probability of B, given A.

Rules of addition

If A and B are mutually exclusive: $P(A ✤ B) = P(A) + P(B)$
If A and B are not mutually exclusive: $P(A ✤ B) = P(A) + P(B) - P(A ∩ B)$

Rules of multiplication

If A and B are independent: $P(A ∩ B) = P(A) * P(B)$
If A and B are not independent: $P(A ∩ B) = P(A) * P(B|A)$
$E(X)$ = expected value = probability * payoff

Quadratic equations

If $aX^2 + bX + c = 0$ is the general quadratic equation, then the two solutions (roots) are given by:

$$X = \frac{-b \pm \sqrt{b^2 - 4ac}}{2a}$$

Descriptive statistics

Arithmetic mean

$$\overline{x} = \frac{\Sigma x}{n}, \overline{x} = \frac{\Sigma fx}{\Sigma f} \text{ (frequency distribution)}$$

Standard deviation

$$SD = \sqrt{\frac{\Sigma(x - \overline{x})^2}{n}}, \quad SD = \sqrt{\frac{\Sigma fx^2}{\Sigma f} - \overline{x}^2} \text{ (frequency distribution)}$$

Index numbers

Price relative $= 100\, P_1/P_0$, Quantity relative $= 100\, Q_1/Q_0$
Price: $\Sigma\, W * P_1/P_0/\Sigma\, W * 100$, where W denotes weights
Quantity: $\Sigma\, W *; Q_1/Q_0/\Sigma\, W * 100$, where W denotes weights

Time series

Additive model
   Series = Trend + Seasonal + Random
Multiplicative model
   Series = Trend * Seasonal * Random

Linear regression and correlation

The linear regression equation of y on x is given by:

$$Y = a + bX \quad \text{or} \quad Y - \overline{Y} = b(X - \overline{X})$$

where

$$b = \frac{\text{Covariance }(XY)}{\text{Variance }(X)} = \frac{n\Sigma XY - (\Sigma X)(\Sigma Y)}{n\Sigma X^2 - (\Sigma X)^2}$$

and

$$a = \overline{Y} - b\overline{X}$$

or solve

$$\Sigma Y = na + b\Sigma X$$

$$\Sigma XY = a\Sigma X + b\Sigma X^2$$

Coefficient of correlation

$$r = \frac{\text{Covariance } (XY)}{\sqrt{\text{Var } (X) \cdot \text{Var } (Y)}} = \frac{n\Sigma XY - (\Sigma X)(\Sigma Y)}{\sqrt{(n\Sigma X^2 - (\Sigma X)^2)(n\Sigma Y^2 - (\Sigma Y)^2)}}$$

$$R \text{ (rank)} = 1 - \frac{6\Sigma d^2}{n\,(n^2 - 1)}$$

Financial mathematics

Compound interest (Values and Sums)

Future value of S, of a sum X, invested for n periods, compounded at $r\%$ interest

$$S = X[1+r]^n$$

Annuity

Present value of an annuity of £1 per annum receivable or payable for n years, commencing in one year, discounted at $r\%$ per annum.

$$PV = \frac{1}{r}\left[1 - \frac{1}{[1 + r]^n}\right]$$

Perpetuity

Present value of £1 per annum, payable or receivable in perpetuity, commencing in one year, discounted at $r\%$ per annum.

$$PV = \frac{1}{r}$$

Note: Logarithm tables are also available when you sit for your assessment.

Mathematical Tables

AREA UNDER THE NORMAL CURVE

This table gives the area under the normal curve between the mean and a point Z standard deviations above the mean. The corresponding area for deviations below the mean can be found by symmetry.

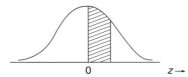

$Z = \dfrac{(x - \mu)}{\sigma}$	0.00	0.01	0.02	0.03	0.04	0.05	0.06	0.07	0.08	0.09
0.0	.0000	.0040	.0080	.0120	.0159	.0199	.0239	.0279	.0319	.0359
0.1	.0398	.0438	.0478	.0517	.0557	.0596	.0636	.0675	.0714	.0753
0.2	.0793	.0832	.0871	.0910	.0948	.0987	.1026	.1064	.1103	.1141
0.3	.1179	.1217	.1255	.1293	.1331	.1368	.1406	.1443	.1480	.1517
0.4	.1554	.1591	.1628	.1664	.1700	.1736	.1772	.1808	.1844	.1879
0.5	.1915	.1950	.1985	.2019	.2054	.2088	.2123	.2157	.2190	.2224
0.6	.2257	.2291	.2324	.2357	.2389	.2422	.2454	.2486	.2518	.2549
0.7	.2580	.2611	.2642	.2673	.2704	.2734	.2764	.2794	.2823	.2852
0.8	.2881	.2910	.2939	.2967	.2995	.3023	.3051	.3078	.3106	.3133
0.9	.3159	.3186	.3212	.3238	.3264	.3289	.3315	.3340	.3365	.3389
1.0	.3413	.3438	.3461	.3485	.3508	.3531	.3554	.3577	.3599	.3621
1.1	.3643	.3665	.3686	.3708	.3729	.3749	.3770	.3790	.3810	.3830
1.2	.3849	.3869	.3888	.3907	.3925	.3944	.3962	.3980	.3997	.4015
1.3	.4032	.4049	.4066	.4082	.4099	.4115	.4131	.4147	.4162	.4177
1.4	.4192	.4207	.4222	.4236	.4251	.4265	.4279	.4292	.4306	.4319
1.5	.4332	.4345	.4357	.4370	.4382	.4394	.4406	.4418	.4430	.4441
1.6	.4452	.4463	.4474	.4485	.4495	.4505	.4515	.4525	.4535	.4545
1.7	.4554	.4564	.4573	.4582	.4591	.4599	.4608	.4616	.4625	.4633
1.8	.4641	.4649	.4656	.4664	.4671	.4678	.4686	.4693	.4699	.4706
1.9	.4713	.4719	.4726	.4732	.4738	.4744	.4750	.4756	.4762	.4767
2.0	.4772	.4778	.4783	.4788	.4793	.4798	.4803	.4808	.4812	.4817
2.1	.4821	.4826	.4830	.4834	.4838	.4842	.4846	.4850	.4854	.4857
2.2	.4861	.4865	.4868	.4871	.4875	.4878	.4881	.4884	.4887	.4890
2.3	.4893	.4896	.4898	.4901	.4904	.4906	.4909	.4911	.4913	.4916
2.4	.4918	.4920	.4922	.4925	.4927	.4929	.4931	.4932	.4934	.4936
2.5	.4938	.4940	.4941	.4943	.4945	.4946	.4948	.4949	.4951	.4952
2.6	.4953	.4955	.4956	.4957	.4959	.4960	.4961	.4962	.4963	.4964
2.7	.4965	.4966	.4967	.4968	.4969	.4970	.4971	.4972	.4973	.4974
2.8	.4974	.4975	.4976	.4977	.4977	.4978	.4979	.4980	.4980	.4981
2.9	.4981	.4982	.4983	.4983	.4984	.4984	.4985	.4985	.4986	.4986
3.0	**.49865**	.4987	.4987	.4988	.4988	.4989	.4989	.4989	.4990	.4990
3.1	**.49903**	.4991	.4991	.4991	.4992	.4992	.4992	.4992	.4993	.4993
3.2	**.49931**	.4993	.4994	.4994	.4994	.4994	.4994	.4995	.4995	.4995
3.3	**.49952**	.4995	.4995	.4996	.4996	.4996	.4996	.4996	.4996	.4997
3.4	**.49966**	.4997	.4997	.4997	.4997	.4997	.4997	.4997	.4997	.4998
3.5	**.49977**									

PRESENT VALUE TABLE

Present value of £1 is $(1 + r)^{-n}$ where r = interest rate; n = number of periods until payment or receipt.

Periods (n)	\multicolumn{20}{c}{Interest rates (r)}																		
	1%	2%	3%	4%	5%	6%	7%	8%	9%	10%	11%	12%	13%	14%	15%	16%	17%	18%	19%	20%
1	.990	.980	.971	.962	.952	.943	.935	.926	.917	.909	.901	.893	.885	.877	.870	.862	.855	.847	.840	.833
2	.980	.961	.943	.925	.907	.890	.873	.857	.842	.826	.812	.797	.783	.769	.756	.743	.731	.718	.706	.694
3	.971	.942	.915	.889	.864	.840	.816	.794	.772	.751	.731	.712	.693	.675	.658	.641	.624	.609	.593	.579
4	.961	.924	.888	.855	.823	.792	.763	.735	.708	.683	.659	.636	.613	.592	.572	.552	.534	.516	.499	.482
5	.951	.906	.863	.822	.784	.747	.713	.681	.650	.621	.593	.567	.543	.519	.497	.476	.456	.437	.419	.402
6	.942	.888	.837	.790	.746	.705	.666	.630	.596	.564	.535	.507	.480	.456	.432	.410	.390	.370	.352	.335
7	.933	.871	.813	.760	.711	.665	.623	.583	.547	.513	.482	.452	.425	.400	.376	.354	.333	.314	.296	.279
8	.923	.853	.789	.731	.677	.627	.582	.540	.502	.467	.434	.404	.376	.351	.327	.305	.285	.266	.249	.233
9	.914	.837	.766	.703	.645	.592	.544	.500	.460	.424	.391	.361	.333	.308	.284	.263	.243	.225	.209	.194
10	.905	.820	.744	.676	.614	.558	.508	.463	.422	.386	.352	.322	.295	.270	.247	.227	.208	.191	.176	.162
11	.896	.804	.722	.650	.585	.527	.475	.429	.388	.350	.317	.287	.261	.237	.215	.195	.178	.162	.148	.135
12	.887	.788	.701	.625	.557	.497	.444	.397	.356	.319	.286	.257	.231	.208	.187	.168	.152	.137	.124	.112
13	.879	.773	.681	.601	.530	.469	.415	.368	.326	.290	.258	.229	.204	.182	.163	.145	.130	.116	.104	.093
14	.870	.758	.661	.577	.505	.442	.388	.340	.299	.263	.232	.205	.181	.160	.141	.125	.111	.099	.088	.078
15	.861	.743	.642	.555	.481	.417	.362	.315	.275	.239	.209	.183	.160	.140	.123	.108	.095	.084	.074	.065
16	.853	.728	.623	.534	.458	.394	.339	.292	.252	.218	.188	.163	.141	.123	.107	.093	.081	.071	.062	.054
17	.844	.714	.605	.513	.436	.371	.317	.270	.231	.198	.170	.146	.125	.108	.093	.080	.069	.060	.052	.045
18	.836	.700	.587	.494	.416	.350	.296	.250	.212	.180	.153	.130	.111	.095	.081	.069	.059	.051	.044	.038
19	.828	.686	.570	.475	.396	.331	.277	.232	.194	.164	.138	.116	.098	.083	.070	.060	.051	.043	.037	.031
20	.820	.673	.554	.456	.377	.312	.258	.215	.178	.149	.124	.104	.087	.073	.061	.051	.043	.037	.031	.026

CUMULATIVE PRESENT VALUE OF £1

This table shows the present value of £1 per annum, receivable or payable at the end of each year for n years $\dfrac{1-(1+r)^{-n}}{r}$.

Periods (n)	\multicolumn{20}{c}{Interest rates (r)}

Periods (n)	1%	2%	3%	4%	5%	6%	7%	8%	9%	10%	11%	12%	13%	14%	15%	16%	17%	18%	19%	20%
1	.990	.980	.971	.962	.952	.943	.935	.926	.917	.909	.901	.893	.885	.877	.870	.862	.855	.847	.840	.833
2	1.970	1.942	1.913	1.886	1.859	1.833	1.808	1.783	1.759	1.736	1.713	1.690	1.668	1.647	1.626	1.605	1.585	1.566	1.547	1.528
3	2.941	2.884	2.829	2.775	2.723	2.673	2.624	2.577	2.531	2.487	2.444	2.402	2.361	2.322	2.283	2.246	2.210	2.174	2.140	2.106
4	3.902	3.808	3.717	3.630	3.546	3.465	3.387	3.312	3.240	3.170	3.102	3.037	2.974	2.914	2.855	2.798	2.743	2.690	2.639	2.589
5	4.853	4.713	4.580	4.452	4.329	4.212	4.100	3.993	3.890	3.791	3.696	3.605	3.517	3.433	3.352	3.274	3.199	3.127	3.058	2.991
6	5.795	5.601	5.417	5.242	5.076	4.917	4.767	4.623	4.486	4.355	4.231	4.111	3.998	3.889	3.784	3.685	3.589	3.498	3.410	3.326
7	6.728	6.472	6.230	6.002	5.786	5.582	5.389	5.206	5.033	4.868	4.712	4.564	4.423	4.288	4.160	4.039	3.922	3.812	3.706	3.605
8	7.652	7.325	7.020	6.733	6.463	6.210	5.971	5.747	5.535	5.335	5.146	4.968	4.799	4.639	4.487	4.344	4.207	4.078	3.954	3.837
9	8.566	8.162	7.786	7.435	7.108	6.802	6.515	6.247	5.995	5.759	5.537	5.328	5.132	4.946	4.772	4.607	4.451	4.303	4.163	4.031
10	9.471	8.983	8.530	8.111	7.722	7.360	7.024	6.710	6.418	6.145	5.889	5.650	5.426	5.216	5.019	4.833	4.659	4.494	4.339	4.192
11	10.368	9.787	9.253	8.760	8.306	7.887	7.499	7.139	6.805	6.495	6.207	5.938	5.687	5.453	5.234	5.029	4.836	4.656	4.486	4.327
12	11.255	10.575	9.954	9.385	8.863	8.384	7.943	7.536	7.161	6.814	6.492	6.194	5.918	5.660	5.421	5.197	4.988	4.793	4.611	4.439
13	12.134	11.348	10.635	9.986	9.394	8.853	8.358	7.904	7.487	7.103	6.750	6.424	6.122	5.842	5.583	5.342	5.118	4.910	4.715	4.533
14	13.004	12.106	11.296	10.563	9.899	9.295	8.745	8.244	7.786	7.367	6.982	6.628	6.302	6.002	5.724	5.468	5.229	5.008	4.802	4.611
15	13.865	12.849	11.938	11.118	10.380	9.712	9.108	8.559	8.061	7.606	7.191	6.811	6.462	6.142	5.847	5.575	5.324	5.092	4.876	4.675
16	14.718	13.578	12.561	11.652	10.838	10.106	9.447	8.851	8.313	7.824	7.379	6.974	6.604	6.265	5.954	5.668	5.405	5.162	4.938	4.730
17	15.562	14.292	13.166	12.166	11.274	10.477	9.763	9.122	8.544	8.022	7.549	7.120	6.729	6.373	6.047	5.749	5.475	5.222	4.990	4.775
18	16.398	14.992	13.754	12.659	11.690	10.828	10.059	9.372	8.756	8.201	7.702	7.250	6.840	6.467	6.128	5.818	5.534	5.273	5.033	4.812
19	17.226	15.679	14.324	13.134	12.085	11.158	10.336	9.604	8.950	8.365	7.839	7.366	6.938	6.550	6.198	5.877	5.584	5.316	5.070	4.843
20	18.046	16.351	14.878	13.590	12.462	11.470	10.594	9.818	9.129	8.514	7.963	7.469	7.025	6.623	6.259	5.929	5.628	5.353	5.101	4.870

Section A

Basic Mathematics

Formulae

Formulae

1

? Concepts, definitions and short-form questions

1   Simplify the following expressions

    (i) $5a + 6b + 2a - 3b$
    (ii) $4x + 3x - 2x - x$
    (iii) $3b + 4c - 2b + 5c$
    (iv) $2a + 3x - 4y + 2a + 2y - 3x$
    (v) $3x + 9y - 4x + 5y - 2z$

2   Expand the following expressions

    (i) $5(2x + 3y - 4z)$
    (ii) $-x(2 + 3x)$
    (iii) $-4(x - 2y + 3z)$
    (iv) $3x(2x - 4y + 3z)$
    (v) $-4y(2y + 4y - 3z)$

3   Simplify the following expressions

    (i) $2a^2 \times a^3$
    (ii) $3a^2 \times 2a^3$
    (iii) $3x^3 \times 12x^4$
    (iv) $(3a^2b)^3$
    (v) $(2a^2x)^2$ when $a = 2$ and $x = 3$

4   Simplify the following expressions

    (i) $x^5 \div x^2$
    (ii) $x^9 \div x^7$
    (iii) $15x^5 \div 3x^4$
    (iv) $a^6 \div a^6$
    (v) $a^5 \div a^7$

5   Calculate the following values

    (i) $3^{0.5}$
    (ii) $2^{0.5}$
    (iii) $4^{1.5}$
    (iv) 10^{-3}
    (v) $36^{-0.5}$

6 Calculate

   (i) $\dfrac{3}{4} + \dfrac{2}{5}$

   (ii) $\dfrac{7}{8} - \dfrac{3}{16}$

   (iii) $\dfrac{1}{3} \times \dfrac{1}{5}$

   (iv) $\dfrac{3}{4} \div \dfrac{2}{5}$

   (v) $1\frac{5}{7} + 3\frac{2}{3}$

7 Given $y = \log_a(x)$

   (i)   What is 'a' called?
   (ii) What is 'x' called?

8 In the formula $Q = \sqrt{\dfrac{2DC}{PR}}$ If $C = 10, P = 6, R = 0.2, D = 600$

   What is the value of Q?

9 In the formula $Q = \sqrt{\dfrac{2CD}{H}}$ If $C = £20, D = 24{,}000, H = £6$

   What is the value of Q?

10 State whether the following statements are true or false.

   (i)   It does not matter in which order multiplications are carried out if there are brackets shown.
   (ii)   The top of a fraction is called the denominator.
   (iii) The bottom of a fraction is called the numerator.
   (iv)   When two or more powers of the same number are multiplied, the individual indices must be added.
   (v)   The decimal fraction of a log number is called the mantissa.
   (vi)   The whole number of a log is called the characteristic.
   (vii) The cube root of 64 is 4.
   (viii) A negative index is calculated by taking the inverse of the number.
   (ix)   15/8 is a larger number than 1.75.
   (x)   The numerical value of $\dfrac{(x^3)^3}{x^7}$ when $x = 5$ is 25

✓ Concepts, definitions and short-form solutions

1   (i) $(5 + 2)a + (6 - 3)b = 7a + 3b$
    (ii) $(4 + 3 - 2 - 1)x = 4x$
    (iii) $3b + 4c - 2b + 5c = b + 9c$
    (iv) $(2 + 2)a + (3 - 3)x + (-4 + 2)y = 4a - 2y$
    (v) $(3 - 4)x + (9 + 5)y + -2z = -x + 14y - 2z$

2   (i) $10x + 15y - 20z$
    (ii) $-2x - 3x^2$
    (iii) $-4x + 8y - 12z$
    (iv) $6x^2 - 12xy + 9xz$
    (v) $-8y^2 - 16y^2 + 12yz$

3   (i) $2 \times a^{(2+3)} = 2a^5$

    (ii) $3 \times 2 \times a^{(2+3)} = 6a^5$

    (iii) $3 \times 12 \times x^{(3+4)} = 36x^7$

    (iv) $3^3 \times (a^2)^3 \, x \, b^3 = 27a^6b^3$

    (v) $(2a^2x)^2 = 2^2 \times 2^4 \times 3^2 = 4 \times 16 \times 9 = 576$

4   (i) $x^{(5-2)} = x^3$

    (ii) $x^{(9-7)} = x^2$

    (iii) $5x^{(5-4)} = 5x$

    (iv) $a^{(6-6)} = a^0 = 1$

    (v) $a^{(5-7)} = a^{-2} = 1/a^2$

5   (i) $\sqrt{3} = 1.732$

    (ii) $\sqrt{2} = 1.414$

    (iii) $\left(\sqrt{4}\right)^3 = \sqrt{64} = 8$

    (iv) $\dfrac{1}{10^3} = \dfrac{1}{1,000} = 0.001$

    (v) $\dfrac{1}{\sqrt{36}} = \dfrac{1}{6}$

6   (i) $\dfrac{15}{20} + \dfrac{8}{20} = \dfrac{23}{20} = 1\dfrac{3}{20}$

    (ii) $\dfrac{14}{16} - \dfrac{3}{16} = \dfrac{11}{16}$

    (iii) $\dfrac{1}{3} \times \dfrac{1}{5} = \dfrac{1}{15}$

    (iv) $\dfrac{3}{4} \times \dfrac{5}{2} = \dfrac{15}{8} = 1\frac{7}{8}$

    (v) $1\frac{15}{21} + 3\frac{14}{21} = 5\frac{8}{21}$

7   (i)   the base

    (ii)   the argument

8   $\dfrac{\sqrt{2 \times 600 \times 10}}{6 \times 0.2} = 100$

   so $Q = 100$

9   $\dfrac{\sqrt{2 \times £20 \times 24,000}}{£6} = 400$

   so $Q = 400$

10   (i)   false

    (ii)   false

    (iii) false

    (iv) true

    (v)   true

    (vi) true

    (vii) true

    (viii) true

    (ix) true

    (x)   true

? Multiple choice questions

1   $6a + 6b + 2a - 3b$ is equal to

    A $6a + 3b$
    B $12ab - 6ab$
    C $12a - 18b$
    D $8a + 3b$

2   $3a^3 \times 4a^4$ is equal to

    A $12a^7$
    B $12a^{12}$
    C $7a^7$
    D $7a^{12}$

3   The number 8^{-2} is equal to

    A -16
    B 6
    C $\sqrt{8}$
    D $\dfrac{1}{64}$

4   The number $36^{-0.5}$ is equal to

    A 18
    B 9
    C 6
    D $\dfrac{1}{6}$

5   In the statement
   $Z < X < Y$ which of the following statements is incorrect?

    A Z is greater than X but less than Y
    B Y is greater than both X and Z
    C X is greater than Z
    D Z is lower than both X and Y

6   The antilog of 261×3.964 is

    A $0{\cdot}261$
    B $0{\cdot}3964$
    C $2{\cdot}4166$
    D $3{\cdot}0147$

7   The statement XY is equivalent to

    A X is less than Y
    B X is less than or equal to Y
    C X is greater than Y
    D X is greater than or equal to Y

8   If $a = 2$ and $b = 3$, $x = 7$ and $y = 8$

then $\dfrac{a}{x} + \dfrac{b}{y}$ is equal to

A $\dfrac{37}{56}$

B $\dfrac{2}{9}$

C $\dfrac{14}{28}$

D $\dfrac{5}{15}$

9   The numeric value of the expression

$\dfrac{(x^3)^3}{x}$ when $x = 5$ is

A   0
B   5
C   25
D   125

10   Which of the following operations will not affect the order in which the numbers appear?

A   addition and multiplication
B   addition and subtraction
C   subtraction and division
D   division and multiplication

✓ Multiple choice solutions

1   $6a + 6b + 2a - 3b$ is equal to $8a + 3b$.
so D

2   We need to multiply the numbers and add the powers so $3a^3 + 4a^4 = 12a^7$.
so A

3   $8^{-2} = \dfrac{1}{8^2} = \dfrac{1}{64}$
so D

4   $36^{-0.5} = \dfrac{1}{\sqrt{36}} = \dfrac{1}{6}$
so D

5   Statement A is incorrect since Z is less than both X and Y.
so A

6   log 261 $= 2.4166$
log 3.964 $= 0.5981$ add
3.0147
so D

7   If $X \leq Y$, this implies that X is less than or equal to Y.
    so B

8   $\dfrac{2}{7} + \dfrac{3}{8} = \dfrac{16}{56} + \dfrac{21}{56} = \dfrac{37}{56}$

    so A

    Note: 2/7   multiplied by 8 to get LCD
              3/8   multiplied by 7 to get LCD

9   A similar question to Q2, top equation becomes x^9, so $\dfrac{x^9}{x^7} = x^2$

    if $x = 5$ then $x^2 = 25$
    so C

10 Addition and multiplication do not affect the order in which the numbers appear.
    so A

Percentages, Ratios and Proportions

Percentages, Ratios and Proportions

2

? Concepts, definitions and short-form questions

1   If VAT is levied on goods and services at $17\frac{1}{2}\%$, how much VAT is paid on goods costing VAT inclusive?

   (i)   £117.50
   (ii) £150
   (iii) £200
   (iv) £250
   (v) £500

2   Equipment is sold for £240 and the cost price is £200. Calculate

   (i)   the gross profit.
   (ii) the profit mark up.

3   If sales are £500 and gross profit is £200, express the gross profit as

   (i)   a fraction
   (ii) a decimal
   (iii) a percentage
   (iv) a ratio

4   James, Fred and Martin are in a business partnership and over the past year have made a profit of £50,000. They have agreed to split profit in the ratio of 5:7:8. How much profit is awarded to

   (i)   James
   (ii) Fred
   (iii) Martin

5   Three balls (red, white and blue) are put into a bag. How many different ways are there of pulling the balls out?

6   Company Y offers its customers a 12% discount on all orders over £500 and 15% on all orders over £1,000. If customer A spends £1,200 and customer B £650, how much discount do they end up giving away?

13

7   State whether the following statements are true or false.

  (i)   To convert a fraction into a % multiply by 100.

  (ii) A proportion cannot be measured as a decimal.

  (iii) If 8 dogs are picked for the final of a dog show, and 3 are to be picked 1st, 2nd and 3rd, There are 500 possible results.

  (iv) A person pays £228 for goods having received a discount of 5%. The undiscounted price was £250.

  (v) $x\%$ of $300 = 3x$

  (vi) An article is sold for £300 VAT inclusive. The vendor receives £300 which is credited to sales.

✓ Concepts, definitions and short-form solutions

1   (i)   £17.50
    (ii) £22.34
    (iii) £29.78
    (iv) £37.23
    (v)   £74.46

2   Gross profit and mark-up are both £40 but margins are different.

$$GP = \frac{40}{240} = \frac{1}{6}$$

$$\text{Mark up} = \frac{40}{200} = \frac{1}{5}$$

3   (i) $\dfrac{200}{500} = \dfrac{2}{5}$

    (ii) .4

    (iii) 40%

    (iv) 4:10

4   James $\dfrac{5}{20} = £12,500$

    Fred $\dfrac{7}{20} = £17,500$

    Martin $\dfrac{8}{20} = £20,000$

5 | | | |
    |---|---|---|
    | Red | White | Blue |
    | Red | Blue | White |
    | White | Red | Blue |
    | White | Blue | Red |
    | Blue | Red | White |
    | Blue | White | Red |

6   Customer A discount 15% of 1,200 =   180
    Customer B discount 12% of 650   =   78
    Total discount given   = £258

7   (i)   true
    (ii) false
    (iii) false

(iv) false
 (v) true
(vi) false

? Multiple choice questions

1 Equipment is sold for £240 and makes a profit of 20% on cost. What is the profit price?

A £10
B £20
C £30
D £40

2 If sales are £500 per week and cost of sales are £300 per week, gross profit expressed as a percentage is

A 10%
B 20%
C 30%
D 40%

3 Alex, Dave and John are in partnership and profits are split in the ratio 7:6:5. If profit for the year is £36,000, how much does Alex receive?

A £10,000
B £12,000
C £14,000
D £16,000

4 If the population of Westend on Sea is 278,000 and 54,000 are of school age, what proportion of the population is of school age?

A 15%
B 19%
C 23%
D 28%

5 An article in a sales catalogue is priced at £298 including VAT at 17.5%. The ex-VAT price of the product is

A £247.34
B £253.62
C £255.00
D £280.50

6 $x\%$ of 200 equals

A $\dfrac{x}{200}$
B $x^{1/2}$
C $200 - x$
D $2x$

7   What is the value of 10.37951 to two decimal places?

   A   10.4
   B   10.3
   C   10.37
   D   10.38

8   Three years ago Smith Bros. purchased a van for £12,000. If they depreciate the vehicle by 25% on a reducing balance basis, the value of the vehicle at the end of year 3 is

   A   £6,000
   B   £5,550.75
   C   £5,062.50
   D   £4,750.25

9   An audit team is made up of a manager, two seniors and four juniors. If there are 10 managers, 15 seniors and 20 juniors how many different audit teams could be formed from these numbers?

   A   20
   B   505,325
   C   5,087,250
   D   impossible to determine

10   City and United play each other twice over the season. Using the terms win, draw and lose, how many permutations are there in the results for the games?

   A   2
   B   6
   C   9
   D   12

✓ Multiple choice solutions

1   If cost price = 100%
   then selling price is 120% of cost
   120% of cost = £240

   $$100\% \text{ of cost} = 240 \times \frac{100}{120}$$

   $$= £200$$

   Profit = £240 − £200 = £40

   so D

2   Gross profit = $\dfrac{£200}{£500}$ = 40%

   so D

3   Total profit to be distributed = £36,000

   Alex receives $\dfrac{7}{18} \times £36,000 = £14,000$

   so C

4   $\dfrac{54{,}000}{278{,}000} = \dfrac{27}{139} = 19\%$

so B

5   Ex VAT price $= \dfrac{£298}{117.5} \times 100 = £253.62$

so B

6   Suppose $x = 10\%$
10% of 100 = 10
10% of 200 = 20
So $x\%$ of 200 is $2x$ of 100
so D

7   We can eliminate A and B since they only go to one decimal place. At three decimal places 0.379 is closer to 0.38 than 0.37.
so D

8   *Depreciation*

Value year 1	9,000	3,000
Value year 2	6,750	2,250
Value year 3	5,062.50	1,687.50

so C

9   No. of managers $= 10$

No. of seniors $= \dfrac{15 \times 14}{2 \times 1} = 105$

No. of assistants $= \dfrac{20 \times 19 \times 18 \times 17}{4 \times 3 \times 2 \times 1} = 4{,}845$

Therefore number of different audit teams $= 10 \times 105 \times 4{,}845$
$= 5{,}087{,}250$

so C

10   *Ist game*   *2nd game*

City	United	City	United
won	lost	lost	won
won	lost	won	lost
won	lost	draw	draw
draw	draw	lost	won
draw	draw	won	lost
draw	draw	draw	draw
lost	won	lost	won
lost	won	won	lost
lost	won	draw	draw

$= 9$
so C

Accuracy
and Rounding

Accuracy and Rounding

3

? Concepts, definitions and short-form questions

1 Complete the following phrase or sentence.

   (i)   A .... variable is one that can assume any value.

   (ii) A .... variable is one that can only assume certain values.

   (iii) An .... variable is one which is not affected by changes in another.

   (iv) A .... variable is affected by changes in another.

   (v) When individuals are rounded in the same direction, this is a .... error.

   (vi) When individuals are rounded in either direction this is an .... error.

2 Calculate $32.6 + 4.32$ and the error if the figures have been rounded to three significant figures.

3 Calculate $32.6 - 4.32$ and the error if the figures have been rounded to three significant figures.

4 Calculate 32.6×4.32 and the error if the figures have been rounded to three significant figures.

5 A product priced at £56.99 has been reduced to £52.49. To two decimal places, the percentage reduction in price is?

✓ Concepts, definitions and short-form solutions

1   (i)   continuous
   (ii) discrete
   (iii) independent
   (iv) dependent
   (v) biased
   (vi) unbiased

2 $(32.6 \pm 0.05) + (4.32 \pm 0.05) = 36.82$

3 $(32.6 \pm 0.05) - (4.32 \pm 0.05) = 28.28$

4   Highest = 32.65 × 4.325 = 141.211
    Lowest = 32.55 × 4.315 = 140.453
    so 140.83 ± 0.38

5   $\dfrac{56.99 - 52.49}{56.99} \times 100 = 7.90\%$

? Multiple choice questions

1   A biased error arises when

    A   individual items are rounded in the same direction
    B   individual items are rounded in either direction
    C   individual items are rounded in the opposite direction
    D   individual items are not rounded

2   An unbiased error arises when

    A   individual items are rounded in the same direction
    B   individual items are rounded in either direction
    C   individual items are rounded in the opposite direction
    D   individual items are not rounded

3   A product was priced at £117.58 and has been reduced to £105.26. To two decimal places the percentage reduction in price was

    A   9.52%
    B   9.93%
    C   10.00%
    D   10.48%

✓ Multiple choice solutions

1   A biased error arises when individual items are rounded in the same direction.
    so A

2   An unbiased error arises when individual items are rounded in either direction.
    so B

3   $\dfrac{£117.58 - £105.26}{£117.58} \times 100 = 10.48\%$

    so D

4

Equations
and Graphs

Equations and Graphs

4

1 Solve the following equations

    (i) $3x + 4y = 25$ $4x + 5y = 32$
    (ii) $x + y = 10$ $x - 4y = 0$
    (iii) $2x + 3y = 42$ $5x - y = 20$
    (iv) $\dfrac{x}{3} + \dfrac{y}{2} = 7$ $\dfrac{2x}{3} - \dfrac{y}{6} = 7$

2 Factorise the following expressions

    (i) $am + bm + an + bn$
    (ii) $12a^2m^3 - 15am^5$
    (iii) $x^2 + 4x - 12$
    (iv) $10p^2 + 11pq - 6q^2$
    (v) $3x^2 + 6x$

3 Quadratic equations. Solve the following

    (i) $9x^2 - 30x + 25 = 0$
    (ii) $3x^2 - 20x + 15 = 40$
    (iii) $x^2 + 6x + 9 = 25$

? Questions 5, 6, 7 and 8 are based on the following data

The group economist believes that if their new product was priced at £100 they will sell 500 units per week.

If price was £50, they would sell 800 units per week. The production department has overheads of £10,000 per week and variable cost per unit is £7.50 per unit.

5 If the quantity is denoted by 'q', derive an expression for the Total Cost in terms of q.

6 If the number of units is denoted by 'x', derive an expression for the Total Revenue in terms of x.

7 Hence derive an expression for the Profit P, in terms of x.

8 At what output is profit maximised?

9 Solve the following by factorisation if possible, otherwise use the formula.

    (i) $x^2 - 5x + 6 = 0$
    (ii) $x^2 + 6x + 7 = 0$

 (iii) $x^2 - 6x + 9 = 0$
 (iv) $2x^2 - 5x + 20 = 0$

10 State whether the following statements are true or false?

  (i) In the equation $y = a + bx$, y is the dependant variable.
  (ii) The shape of a linear demand curve is a straight line.
  (iii) Quadratic equations can never be solved by factorisation.
  (iv) If $b^2 - 4ac$ is zero, there is only one solution to the equation.
  (v) If $b^2 - 4ac$ is positive, there are no real solutions.
  (vi) If $x + y = 9$ then both x and y must be positive.

  (vii) The formula used to solve quadratic equations is $x = \dfrac{-b \pm \sqrt{(b^2 - 4ac)}}{2a}$.

  (viii) Quadratic equations cannot be solved by using a graph.

✓ Concepts, definitions and short-form solutions

1 (i) $3x + 4y = 25$ multiply by 4 (1)
   $4x + 5y = 32$ multiply by 3 (2)
   $12x + 16y = 100$
   $12x + 15y = 96$
   subtracting (1) from (2) becomes $y = 4$
   $3x + 16 = 25$
     $x = 3$
   so $x = 3, y = 4$

 (ii) $\dfrac{x}{3} + \dfrac{y}{2} = 7$ $\dfrac{2x}{3} - \dfrac{y}{6} = 7$
   multiply everything by 6
   $2x + 3y = 42$ (1)
   $4x - y = 42$ (2)
   multiply equation (2) by 3
   $2x + 3y = 42$
   $12x - 3y = 126$
   $14x = 168$
    $x = 12$
   If $x = 12$, then $y = 6$

2 $2x + 3y + 4z = 9$ (1)
 $3x - 2y - 3z = 3$ (2)
 $4x + 5y - 2z = 25$ (3)
 Step 1 − eliminate x
 $6x + 9y + 12z = 27$ equation (1) × 3
 $6x - 4y - 6z = 6$ equation (2) × 2
 subtract $13y + 18z = 21$ (4)
 $4x + 6y + 8z = 18$ equation (1) × 2
 $4x + 5y - 2z = 25$ (3)
 subtract $y + 10z = -7$ (5)
 multiply equation (5) by 13
 $13y + 130z = -91$ (6)
 $13y + 18z = 21$

$$112z = -112$$
$$z = -1$$
$$y + 10z = -7$$
$$y - 10 = -7$$
$$y = -7 + 10$$
$$y = 3$$
$$2x + 3y + 4z = 9$$
$$2x + 9 - 4 = 9$$
$$2x = 4$$
$$x = 2$$
solution $x = 2, y = 3, z = -1$

3 (i) $m(a + b) + n(a + b)$
   (ii) $3am^3(4a - 5m^2)$
   (iii) $(x + 6)(x - 2)$
   (iv) $(5p - 2q)(2p + 3q)$
   (v) $3x(x + 2)$

4 (i) $-(-30) \pm \sqrt{\dfrac{(-30)^2 - 4 \times 9 \times 25}{2 \times 9}} = 0$

$$= \frac{30 \pm \sqrt{0}}{18} = \frac{5}{3}$$

   (ii) $-(-20) \pm \sqrt{\dfrac{(-20)^2 - 4 \times 3 \times 15}{2 \times 9}} = 0$

$$= \frac{20 \pm \sqrt{220}}{18} = \frac{20 \pm 14.83}{18} = 20.82 \text{ or } 19.18$$

   (iii) $-6 \pm \dfrac{\sqrt{6^2 - 4 \times 1 \times 9}}{2 \times 1} = 0$

$$= -6 \pm \frac{\sqrt{0}}{2} = -3$$

5 Total cost = £10,000 + 7.5q

6 Let price per unit be £p/unit
   when $x = 500$ $p = 100$ $500 = a + bp$
   when $x = 800$ $p = 50$ $800 = a + bp$
$$500 = a + 100b$$
$$800 = a + 50b$$
$$300 = -50b$$
$$b = -6$$
$$500 = a + 100 \times (-6)$$
$$500 = a - 600$$
$$a = 1,100$$
$$x = 1,100 - 6p$$
$$6p = 1,100 - x$$
$$p = \frac{1,100 - x}{6} = 183.33 - \frac{x}{6}$$
Sales revenue = $p \times x$
$$\text{so } R = x\left(183.33 - \frac{x}{6}\right)$$
$$R = 183.33x - \frac{x^2}{6}$$

7   Profit $= R - T$

$$= \left(183x - \frac{x^2}{6}\right) - (10{,}000 + 7.5x)$$

8   Profit is maximised where marginal cost = marginal revenue.

9   (i)   Factorise $x = 2$ or 3
    (ii) Does not factorise $x = -1.59$ or -4.41
    (iii) Factorises $x = 3$ twice
    (iv) Does not factorise $x = 2.15$ or 4.65

10   (i)   true
        (ii)   true
        (iii)   false
        (iv)   true
        (v)   false
        (vi)   false
        (vii)   true
        (viii) false

❓ Multiple choice questions

1   A square-ended rectangular box has a volume of 1,458 cm³. The length of the box is twice that of one side of the square end. One side of the square end measures

   A   6 cm
   B   9 cm
   C   18 cm
   D   24 cm

❓ Questions 2, 3 and 4 are based on the following information

The marketing department estimates that if the selling price of the new product is set at £40 per unit, sales will be 400 units per week. If the selling price is £20 per unit, sales will be 800 units per week. The production department estimates that variable costs will be £7.50 per unit and fixed costs £10,000 per week.

2   The cost equation is

   A   £10,000 + £7.5x
   B   £10,000 − £7.5x
   C   £10,000 + £40
   D   £10,000 + £75x

3   The sales revenue equation is

   A $400 - 9$
   B $1{,}200 - 9$
   C $60x - \dfrac{x^2}{20}$
   D $60x - x^2$

4   The profit equation is

A $-\dfrac{x^2}{20} + 52.5x - 10{,}000$

B $-x + 52.5 - 10{,}000$

C $x^2 - 52.5x + 10{,}000$

D $x^2 - 52.5x - 10{,}000$

5   If $3x + 4y = 25$ and $10x + 2y = 38$ what are the values of x and y?

A $x = 3 \quad y = 3$

B $x = 3 \quad y = 4$

C $x = 4 \quad y = 5$

D $x = 5 \quad y = 4$

6   If $9x^2 - 30x + 25 = 0$ then x is equal to

A $\dfrac{2}{3}$

B 1

C $\dfrac{5}{3}$

D 2

7   The shape of a graph of linear equation will be

A   U shape

B   straight line

C   L shape

D   depends on the linear equation

8   For the equation $ax^2 + bx + c = 0$, if $b^2 - 4ac$ is positive then

A   there is only one solution

B   there are two possible solutions

C   there are no real solutions

D   impossible to determine without knowing their values

9   In the equations $2x + 3y + 4z = 9$

$3x - 2y - 3z = 3$

$4x + 5y - 2z = 25$

the values of x, y and z are

A $x = 2 \quad y = 3 \quad z = -1$

B $x = 1 \quad y = 3 \quad z = 2$

C $x = 2 \quad y = 1 \quad z = 3$

D $x = 3 \quad y = 2 \quad z = 1$

10   If $6x^2 + 12x = 4(5x + 2)$ then the values of x are

A $\dfrac{-2}{3}$ or 2

B $\dfrac{-3}{2}$ or 1

C $\dfrac{-3}{2}$ or 1

D $\dfrac{2}{3}$ or 2

✓ Multiple choice solutions

1   Volume of rectangular box is equal to length × height × depth.
$1{,}458 = 2x \times x \times x$
$1{,}458 = 2x^3$
$729 \quad = x^3$
$\sqrt[3]{729} = x$
$\qquad x = 9$
so B

2   Total cost = Fixed cost + Variable cost
$\qquad\qquad = \pounds10{,}000 + \pounds7.5x$
so A

3   $x = a + bp$ since graph of this function is linear
when $x = 400 \quad p = 40$
$400 = a + 40b \quad (1)$
when $x = 800 \quad p = 20$
$800 = a + 20b \quad (2)$
subtracting (1) from (2)
we have $400 = -20b$
$\dfrac{400}{-20} = b$
so $\quad b = -20$
using equation (1)
$400 = a + 40 \times (-20)$
$400 = a - 800$
$400 + 800 = a$
$a = 1{,}200$
so $x = 1{,}200 - 20p$
$20p = 1{,}200 - x$
$p = \dfrac{1{,}200 - x}{20} = 60 - \dfrac{x}{20}$
Sales revenue $= x \times p$
so $x \times \left(60 - \dfrac{x}{20}\right)$
$R = 60x - \dfrac{x^2}{20}$
so C

4   The profit equation is total revenue − total cost
$= \left(60x - \dfrac{x^2}{20}\right) - (10{,}000 + 7.5x)$
$= \dfrac{-x^2}{20} + 52.5x - 10{,}000$
so A

5   $3x + 4y = 25 \quad (1)$
$10x + 2y = 38 \quad (2)$
Multiply equation (2) by 2
$20x + 4y = 76$
$3x + 4y = 25$

$$17x = 51$$
$$x = 3$$
$$3x + 4y = 25$$
$$9 + 4y = 25$$
$$4y = 16$$
$$y = 4$$
so $x = 3$ and $y = 4$
so B

6   Using the formula
$$x = \frac{-b \pm \sqrt{b^2 - 4ac}}{2a}$$
where $a = 9$ $b = -30$ $c = 25$
$$x = \frac{-(-30) \pm \sqrt{900 - 900}}{18}$$
$$= \frac{30 \pm 0}{18}$$
$$= \frac{5}{3}$$
so C

7   The shape of a graph of a linear equation will be a straight line.
so B

8   If $b^2 - 4ac$ is zero, there is only one solution
If $b^2 - 4ac$ is positive, there are two solutions
If $b^2 - 4ac$ is negative, there are no solutions
so B

9   Eliminate x (either of the other variables would do) between (1) and (2):
$3 \times$ (1): $6x + 9y + 12z = 27$
$2 \times$ (2): $6x - 4y - 6z = 6$
Subtract: $13y + 18z = 21$ (4)
Eliminate x between (3) and (1), ((2) could have been used instead of (1)):
$2 \times$ (1): $4x + 6y + 8z = 18$
   (3): $4x + 5y - 2z = 25$
Subtract: $y + 10z = -7$ (5)
Multiply equation (5) by 13
$13y + 130z = -91$ (6)
Subtract (4) from (6)
$13y + 130z = -91$ (6)
$13y + 18z = 21$ (4)
$112z = -112$
Rearrange the equation to obtain a value for z.
$112z = -112$
$$z = \frac{-112}{112}$$
$$z = -1$$

Substitute the value of z into equation (5)

$y + 10z = -7$

$y + 10(-1) = -7$

$y - 10 = -7$

$y = -7 + 10$

$y = 3$

Due to there being three unknowns, substitute the values for y and z into equation (1) to obtain a value for x.

$2x + 3y + 4z = 9$ (1)

$2x + 3 \times (3) + 4 \times (-1) = 9$

$2x + 9 - 4 = 9$

$2x = 9 - 9 + 4$

$2x = 4$

$x = \dfrac{4}{2}$

$x = 2$

Check in either (2) or (3):

from(2): $3 \times 2 - 2 \times 3 - 3 \times (-1) = 3$

$6 - 6 + 3 = 3$

$3 = 3$

Hence the solution is $x = 2, y = 3, z = -1$

so A

10    $6x^2 + 12x = 4(5x + 2)$

$6x^2 + 12x = 20x + 8$

$6x^2 - 8x - 8 = 0$

$x = \dfrac{-(-8) \pm \sqrt{(-8)^2 - (4 \times 6 \times (-8))}}{2 \times 6}$

$= \dfrac{8 \pm \sqrt{64 + 192}}{12}$

$= \dfrac{8}{12} \pm \dfrac{16}{12}$

$x = \dfrac{-2}{3}$ or $x = 2$

so A

Section B

Probability

Probability Theory

Probability Theory   5

[?] Concepts, definitions and short-form questions

1   If a card is pulled out of a pack of playing cards at random what is the probability that it is

   (i)   black
   (ii)   a club
   (iii) an ace
   (iv)   the ace of spades

2   Fill in the missing word

   (i)   Where the probability of an event is calculated by a process of logical reasoning, this is known as .... probability.
   (ii)   When a situation can be repeated a number of times this is classed as .... probability.
   (iii) Where estimates are made by individuals of the relative likelihood of events occurring, this is called .... probability.
   (iv)   A pictorial representation in which terms of a mathematical statement are shown by overlapping circles is known as a .... diagram.

3   City and United play each other twice per season. Each side has an equal chance of winning in a match between them. Frank Green, a local bookmaker, publishes odds of either of the teams to win both games at 5–1. Is Frank expected to lose money with these odds?

4   There are 500 fish in a lake. There are 200 pike, 150 perch, 100 trout and 50 salmon. Each fish has an equal chance of being caught.

   (i)   What is the probability that a pike is caught first?
   (ii)   What is the probability that a pike or a perch is caught first?
   (iii) What is the probability that a pike, perch or salmon is caught first?
   (iv)   What is the probability that a perch is not caught first?
   (v)   What is the probability that neither a salmon nor a trout is caught first?

5   In a room there are 100 CIMA students. Fifty per cent are male and 50% are female. Sixty per cent are fully qualified, 40% are partly qualified. What is the probability of selecting at random a student who is

   (i)   male?
   (ii)   fully qualified?
   (iii) male and qualified?

    (iv)   male or qualified?

    (v)   female or qualified?

6   Twenty-five per cent of new cars of a particular model are supplied from factory X. The remainder come from factory Y. Ten per cent of factory X's output has a major fault whilst 18% of factory Y's output has the same fault.

    (i)   What is the probability that a car selected at random has a major defect?

    (ii)   What is the probability it was made at factory X?

    (iii)   What is the probability it was made at factory Y?

7   A box contains four red balls, two white balls and a yellow ball. If three balls are selected at random and there is no replacement between each selection what is the probability of selecting

    (i)   three of the same colour?

    (ii)   one of each colour?

8   If we toss a fair coin two times

    (i)   what is the probability that first toss is a head?

    (ii)   what is the probability that both tosses will be heads?

    (iii)   what is the probability that neither tosses will be heads?

    (iv)   what is the probability that a head would not appear in three consecutive tosses?

9   A travel agent keeps a stock of holiday brochures. Currently there is a total of 500 brochures in stock, as follows: 285 for European holidays, 90 for American holidays, 110 for Asian holidays and 15 for African holidays. A brochure is selected at random.

Calculate the following probabilities

    (i)   that a European brochure is selected

    (ii)   that an African brochure is NOT selected

    (iii)   that neither an American nor an Asian brochure is selected

    (iv)   that either a European or an Asian brochure is selected

10   What is a mutually exclusive event?

✓ Concepts, definitions and short-form solutions

1   (i) $\dfrac{26}{52} = \dfrac{1}{2}$

    (ii) $\dfrac{13}{52} = \dfrac{1}{4}$

    (iii) $\dfrac{4}{52} = \dfrac{1}{13}$

    (iv) $\dfrac{1}{52} = \dfrac{1}{52}$

2   (i)   a priori

    (ii)   empirical probability

    (iii)   subjective probability

    (iv)   venn

3   He is not too over generous

In match 1 there are three possible outcomes: City win – United win – draw

In match 2 there are also three possible outcomes, so between the two matches there are nine possible outcomes, so the chances of either team beating each other twice is 9 − 1, not good odds.

4   (i)   200 in 500 or 40%
(ii)   200 + 150 in 500 or 70%
(iii)   200 + 150 + 50 in 500 or 80%
(iv)   500 − 150 in 500 or 70%
(v)   500 − (100 + 50) in 500 or 70%

5   (i)   50 in 100 or 50%
(ii)   60 in 100 or 60%
(iii) $\dfrac{50}{100} \times \dfrac{60}{100}$ or 30%
(iv)   Someone who is not male or qualified is female and unqualified. This probability
$= \dfrac{50}{100} \times \dfrac{40}{100} = 20\%$
therefore male or qualified must be 100 − 20% = 80%
(v)   same as (iii) $\dfrac{50}{100} \times \dfrac{60}{100} = 30\%$

6   Where only percentage figures are given, it is easier to use an absolute number such as 1,000 and produce the following table:

	Factory X	Factory Y	Total
Fault	25	135	160
OK	225	615	840
Total	250	750	1,000

(i)   160 in 1,000 or 16%
(ii)   25 in 160 or 16%
(iii)   135 in 160 or 84%

7   There is only one colour which can be selected three times – red
(i)   so $\dfrac{4}{7} \times \dfrac{3}{6} \times \dfrac{2}{5} = \dfrac{24}{210} = \dfrac{4}{35} = 0.1$
(ii)   There are six possible outcomes that give one of each colour

(i)	Red	White	Yellow
(ii)	Red	Yellow	White
(iii)	White	Red	Yellow
(iv)	White	Yellow	Red
(v)	Yellow	Red	White
(vi)	Yellow	White	Red

$$\text{so probability} = 6 \times \frac{4}{7} \times \frac{2}{6} \times \frac{1}{5}$$

$$= \frac{48}{210}$$

$$= \frac{8}{15} = 0.23$$

8   (i)   Probability that first toss is head
= 50 − 50 or 1 in 2

(ii)   Probability
$$= \frac{1}{2} \times \frac{1}{2} = 1 \text{ in } 4$$

(iii)   If neither toss is a head then both must be a tail.
Probability of two tails
$$= \frac{1}{2} \times \frac{1}{2} = 1 \text{ in } 4$$
so chances that neither are heads
= 1 − 1 in 4 = 3 in 4

(iv)   For head not to appear in three consecutive tosses, we would need 3 tails which
$$\text{is} = \frac{1}{2} \times \frac{1}{2} \times \frac{1}{2} = \frac{1}{8}$$
$$\text{so probability} = 1 - \frac{1}{8} = \frac{7}{8}$$

9   (i)   Probability that a European brochure is selected $= \dfrac{285}{500} = 0.57$

(ii)   Probability that an African brochure is not selected
$$= \frac{500 - 15}{500} = \frac{485}{500} = 0.97$$

(iii)   Probability that neither an American nor an Asian brochure is selected
$$= \frac{500 - 90 - 110}{500} = \frac{300}{500} = 0.60$$

(iv)   Probability that either a European or an Asian brochure is selected
$$= \frac{285 + 110}{500} = \frac{395}{500} = 0.79$$

10   *Mutually exclusive events*

Two or more events are said to be mutually exclusive if the occurrence of any one of them precludes the occurrence of all others, that is only one thing can happen. For example if we throw a coin and it lands heads it cannot be a tail.

? Multiple choice questions

Questions 1–4 relate to the following information

A pack of cards consists of 52 playing cards.

1   What is the probability that a card selected at random is the ace of hearts?

   A   1 in 2
   B   1 in 13
   C   1 in 26
   D   1 in 52

2 What is the probability that a card selected at random is an ace?

A 1 in 2
B 1 in 13
C 1 in 26
D 1 in 52

3 What is the probability that a card selected at random is a heart?

A 1 in 2
B 1 in 4
C 1 in 9
D 1 in 13

4 What is the probability that a card selected at random is red?

A 1 in 2
B 1 in 3
C 1 in 4
D 1 in 5

？ Questions 5–8 relate to a number of CIMA students who recently sat for Paper 3c

Type of student	Total number of scripts	Total number of passes
Male	1,000	500
Female	500	300

5 If a student is selected at random what is the probability she is female?

A 1 in 2
B 1 in 3
C 1 in 4
D 1 in 5

6 If a student is selected at random what is the probability that they failed?

A 1 in 2
B 1 in 3
C 7 in 15
D 8 in 15

7 If a student is selected at random what is the probability that the student is male or someone who failed?

A 0.5
B 0.6
C 0.7
D 0.8

8 If a student is selected at random what is the probability of selecting a male who failed?

  A   1 in 2
  B   1 in 3
  C   1 in 4
  D   1 in 5

? Questions 9 and 10 are based on the following

A box contains four red balls, two blue balls and a yellow ball. If three balls are selected at random and there is no replacement between each selection.

9 What is the probability of selecting one of each colour?

  A   0.21
  B   0.23
  C   0.25
  D   0.27

10 What is the probability of selecting three of the same colour?

  A   0.07
  B   0.09
  C   0.11
  D   0.15

✓ Multiple choice solutions

1 There is only one such card in the pack so probability is 1 in 52.
   so D

2 There are four aces in a pack so $\dfrac{4}{52} = \dfrac{1}{13}$.
   so B

3 There are 13 hearts in a pack of 52 so $\dfrac{13}{52}$ or $\dfrac{1}{4}$.
   so B

4 There are 26 red cards in a pack of 52 so $\dfrac{26}{52}$ or $\dfrac{1}{2}$.
   so A

5 Total number of females 500
   Total number of students 1,500 so $\dfrac{500}{1,500} = \dfrac{1}{3}$.
   so B

6 Total number of failures
   Total number of students $\dfrac{700}{1,500}$ so 7 in 15.
   so C

7   Turn question round

Someone who is not male and failed is a female who passed

$$\frac{\text{Total number of females who passed}}{\text{Total number of students}}$$

$$= \frac{300}{1,500} = 1 \text{ in } 5$$

Therefore the opposite = 4 in 5 or 0.8
so D

8   $$\frac{1,000}{1,500} \times \frac{500}{1,000} = \frac{2}{3} \times \frac{1}{2} = \frac{2}{6} \text{ or } \frac{1}{3}$$
so 1 in 3
so B

9   There are six possible ways that give one of each colour

Ball 1	Ball 2	Ball 3
Red	Blue	Yellow
Red	Yellow	Blue
Yellow	Red	Blue
Yellow	Blue	Red
Blue	Red	Yellow
Blue	Yellow	Red

So probability of one of each colour $= 6 \times \dfrac{4}{7} \times \dfrac{2}{6} \times \dfrac{1}{5} = \dfrac{8}{38} = 0.23$

so B

10 Only one colour can be selected three times – red

so chance of 3 reds $= \dfrac{4}{7} \times \dfrac{3}{6} \times \dfrac{2}{5} = \dfrac{4}{35} = 0.11$

so C

6

Expected Value and Decision-Making

Expected Value and Decision-Making

6

? Concepts, definitions and short-form questions

1 The local council are considering purchasing a snow plough which would cost £20,000 per annum. This would save on outside contractors but the amount would depend on the severity of the winter.

Winter	Annual savings	Probability
severe	£40,000	0.2
average	£20,000	0.5
mild	£10,000	0.3

Based on the expected cost due to weather conditions, would you advise the council to buy their own plough?

2 A market trader has the choice of selling umbrellas or ice cream. It has a 60% chance of raining and a 40% chance of being fair. If it rains he will make £200 profit on umbrellas and lose £50 if he chooses ice cream. If it is fair, he will lose £10 selling umbrellas and make £150 selling ice cream. Which product would you advise him to sell?

3 A new product is expected to generate the following profits:

Level of demand	Profits	Probability
high	£100,000	0.1
medium	£50,000	0.5
low	£20,000 loss	0.4

(i) What is the expected profit from the new product?
(ii) What is the maximum you would invest in this product?

4 *Expected values*

A State two advantages of expected values.
B State two disadvantages of expected values.

5 Miss Jones is a supply teacher. Each day she must decide to travel to the agency where there is a 75% chance that she will get work. Her train fare is £10 return.
There are three types of jobs available:

(i) teaching CIMA students for £200 per day
(ii) teaching ACCA students for £150 per day
(iii) teaching Chartered students for £100 per day

The chances of CIMA are 10%, ACCA 40% and Chartered 50%.

Draw a decision tree which shows this information and advise Miss Jones what she should do.

6 A company is deciding between three projects A, B and C. The expected profit from each one is as follows:

Project A		Project B		Project C	
Profit	Probability	Profit	Probability	Profit	Probability
£5,000	0.5	£10,000	0.3	£6,000	0.4
£2,500	0.5	£1,000	0.7	£4,000	0.6

Rank projects in descending order, stating expected values of each.

1

2

3

7 In a forthcoming sales promotion each pack of cigarettes is to contain a leaflet with eight 'scratch off' square patches, randomly arranged. The purchaser will scratch off one patch to reveal the value of a small prize. The value of the eight patches on the leaflet is to be as follows:

Value of prize	£0.20	£0.50	£1
Number of patches	5	2	1

The company has to decide on the number of packs in which to put leaflets, given a budget of £75,000.

Find the 'average cost' of a leaflet, and deduce the number of leaflets you would use and why.

8 In another promotion for cigarettes, a leaflet pictures a roulette wheel with 37 numbers, seven of which are randomly arranged winning numbers. The purchaser is allowed to scratch off seven of the 37 numbers in the hope of winning a prize. It is therefore possible to select 0, 1, 2, 3, 4, 5, 6 or 7 winning numbers on each leaflet.

(i) What is the probability of a purchase not winning a prize?
(ii) If there are one million purchases during the promotion, what are the chances of the 'Super Prize' (the Super Prize is when all seven selections are winners) being won?

9 A golf club has to decide how many programmes to produce for a Charity Pro-Am golf tournament. From previous experience of similar tournaments, it is expected that the probability of sales will be as follows:

Number of programmes demanded	Probability of demand
1,000	0.1
2,000	0.4
3,000	0.2
4,000	0.2
5,000	0.1

The best quotation from a local printer is £2,000 plus 10 pence per copy. Advertising revenue totals £1,500. Programmes are sold for 60 pence each. Unsold programmes are worthless.

Draw up a profit table with programme production levels as columns and programme demand levels as rows.

✓ Concepts, definitions and short-form solutions

1   Cost of new machine = £20,000
Expected saving   = (0.2 × 40,000) + (0.5 × 20,000) + (0.3 × 10,000)
                     = £8,000 + £10,000 + £3,000
                     = £21,000

Based purely on expected value theory, the council should buy a new snow plough since they could save £1,000 more than the machine costs.

2

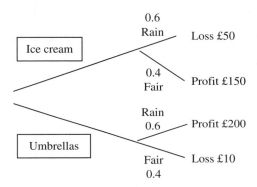

Expected value selling ice cream
= (0.6 × −£50) + 0.4 × (£150) = −£30 + £60 = £30

Expected value selling umbrellas
= (0.6 × £200) + (0.4 × −£10) = £120 + (£4) = £116
so choose umbrellas.

3   (i)   Expected profit from new product is
           (0.1 × £100,000) + (0.5 × £50,000) + (0.4 × −20,000)
           = £10,000 + £25,000 − £8,000
           = £27,000
    (ii) £27,000

4   A   (i)   It is an objective way of making investment decisions.
        (ii) Over the long term, the correct decision will be taken.

    B   (i)   On individual projects the wrong decision may be made because of random events.
        (ii) A 10% chance of winning £1,000 would show a higher expected value than a 90% chance of winning £100 but would it be the correct decision to take?

5

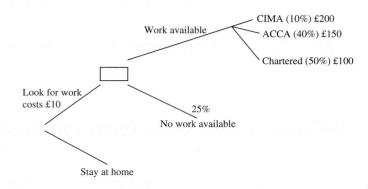

If there is work she can expect

10% of £200 + 40% of £150 + 50% of £100 = £20 + £60 + £50
$$= £130$$

That is only if work is available, so expected value
= 75% × £130 + 25% × 0   = £97.50

However, whether she finds work or not she will still have to pay £10 for train fare so her expected income from work   = £97.50 − £10 = £87.50

If she stays at home her expected value is £0 so advise Miss Jones to seek work.

6   Project A = (0.5 × £5,000) + (0.5 × £2,500)
            = £3,750

Project B = (0.3 × £10,000) + (0.7 × £1,000)
            = £3,700

Project C = (0.4 × £6,000) + (0.6 × £4,000)
            = £4,800
so 1 C
   2 A
   3 B

7   *Cigarette sales promotion*

The average value of a prize is calculated as follows

Value (x) £	Frequency f	fx
0.20	5	1.00
0.50	2	1.00
1.00	1	1.00
	8	3.00

Mean $= \dfrac{\Sigma fx}{\Sigma f} = \dfrac{3.00}{8} = 37.5\text{p}$

Total cost = Average cost per leaflet × no. of leaflets
£75,000   = 0.375 × x

$$x = \frac{£75,000}{0.375} = 200,000$$

So 200,000 leaflets should be used.

8 (i) Probability that first number uncovered is not a winner $= \dfrac{30}{37}$
This would leave 36 numbers and 29 non-winners.

Probability that the second number is not a winner $= \dfrac{29}{36}$
This would leave 35 numbers and 28 non-winners.

Similarly for all 7 numbers, hence

$$P\text{ (no win)} = \frac{30}{37} \times \frac{29}{36} \times \frac{28}{35} \times \frac{27}{34} \times \frac{26}{33} \times \frac{25}{32} \times \frac{24}{31}$$
$$= 0.1977$$

(ii) Probability that first number uncovered is a winner $= \dfrac{7}{37}$
This would leave 36 numbers and 6 winners.

Probability that the second number is a winner $= \dfrac{6}{36}$ etc.

Hence

$$P\text{ (all win)} = \frac{7}{37} \times \frac{6}{36} \times \frac{5}{35} \times \frac{4}{34} \times \frac{3}{33} \times \frac{2}{32} \times \frac{1}{31}$$
$$= 9.713 \times 10^{-8}$$

The expected number of Super Prizes in 1 million cards is $9.713 \times 10^{-8} \times 10^{6}$ (i.e. probability $\times$ no. of cards)
$$= 0.09713$$

This is the probability that the Super Prizes is won in one promotion.

The chance is, therefore 1 in $\dfrac{1}{0.09713}$
$$= 1 \text{ in } 10 \text{ (approximately)}$$

9 Contribution per programme sold is (60p − 10p) = 50p. The table shows expected profits (needed for part (b)) found by working 4.

Demand (probability in brackets)	1,000	2,000	*Production* 3,000	4,000	5,000
1,000 (0.1)	(W$_1$) £0	(W$_2$) £(100)	£(200)	£(300)	£(400)
2,000 (0.4)	£0	(W$_3$) £500	£400	£300	£200
3,000 (0.2)	£0	£500	£1,000	£900	£800
4,000 (0.2)	£0	£500	£1,000	£1,500	£1,400
5,000 (0.1)	£0	£500	£1,000	£1,500	£2,000
Expected £ value	£0	(W$_4$) £440	£640	£720	£680

Workings

		£
(W$_1$) Contribution from sales of 1,000	=	500
Less: (Fixed print cost − Advertising revenue)	=	(500)
		nil
(W$_2$) Contribution from sales of 1,000	=	500
Less		(500)
Less: 1,000 programmes printed and sold @ £0.10	=	(100)
		(100)

(W_3) Contribution from sales of 2,000   = 1,000
     Less   (500)

         500

(W_4) $(0.1 \times 100) + (0.4 \times 500) + (0.2 \times 500) + (0.2 \times 500) + (0.1 \times 500) = £440.$

? Multiple choice questions

1 A retailer has the choice of selling Product A which has a 0.4 chance of high sales and a 0.6 chance of low sales. High sales would yield a profit of £600. Low sales would yield a profit of £100. If Product B was sold there is a 0.6 chance of high sales and a 0.4 chance of low sales which would result in a profit of £400 or a loss of £50. Which product would be chosen and what would be the expected value?

    A   Product A   £300
    B   Product B   £220
    C   Product A   £220
    D   Product B   £300

2 A decision tree is

    A   a way of applying expected value criterion to situations where a number of decisions are made sequentially
    B   a random outcome point
    C   a statistical device used purely for retailers
    D   none of the above

3 The difference between a decision point and a random outcome point is

    A   decision points are where the decision made has no control over destiny
    B   a decision point and a random outcome point are the same
    C   a decision point is chosen by the decision maker, at a random point it is outside the control of the decision maker
    D   none of the above

4 Ten per cent of golf balls have a minor defect. They are packaged in boxes of six. What is the probability that a box selected at random has no defects?

    A   0.41
    B   0.45
    C   0.51
    D   0.53

5 If the three possible outcomes of a decision are profits of £10, £50 and £80 with probabilities of 0.3, 0.3 and 0.4, what is the expected profit?

    A   £40
    B   £44
    C   £47
    D   £50

6   A supermarket is opening a new store and they have identified two sites A and B with 0.8 chance of making £400,000 profit per annum and a 0.2 chance of incurring an £80,000 loss. The expected value of those sites is

A   £300,000
B   £302,000
C   £304,000
D   £306,000

7   A newspaper vendor buys daily newspapers each day which have a resale value at the end of the day of zero. He buys the papers for 15p and sells them for 30p. The levels of demand per day and their associated probabilities are as follows

Demand per day	Probability
400	0.2
440	0.3
480	0.4
520	0.1

How many newspapers should the vendor buy each day?

A   400
B   440
C   480
D   520

8   A social club has a lottery draw based on numbers between 1 and 40. If they pay £50 for the winning number and there are no other expenses how much will they need to sell each ticket for in order to make £50 profit?

A   £2
B   £2.50
C   £3
D   not enough information given

9   If a roulette table has 37 numbers 0–36 and pays odds of 35–1 on punters guessing the correct number, what is the expected rate of return on a £100 investment?

A   −5%
B   +5%
C   95%
D   100%

10 A new car is worth £20,000. The probability of this car being stolen or being involved in an accident over a year is 1%.

The driver pays an insurance policy of £500 per annum. The annual expected value to the insurance company is

A   £500
B   £400
C   £300
D   £200

✓ Multiple choice solutions

1   Product A expected value
    $= 0.4 \times £600 + 0.6 \times £100 = £240 + £60 = £300$

    Product B expected value
    $= 0.6 \times £400 + 0.4 \times -£50 = £240 - £20 = £220$

    Product A with higher expected value
    so A

2   A decision tree is a way of applying expected value criterion to situations where a number of decisions are made sequentially.
    so A

3   A decision point is where the decision maker can make a choice. A random outcome point is outside the control of the decision maker.
    so C

4   Probability of having 0 defects is $\dfrac{(9)^6}{10} = 0.53$
    so D

5   $\dfrac{0.3}{£10} + \dfrac{0.3}{£50} + \dfrac{0.4}{£80}$ $= £3 + £15 + £32$

    $= £50$
    so D

6   $\dfrac{0.8}{£400,000} - \dfrac{0.2}{£80,000} = £320,000 - £1,600$

    $= £304,000$
    so C

7   If the newsagent purchased and sold 400 papers per day, his profit would be £60 (400 × 15p).

    If the newsagent buys 400 but demand is 440 profit is still only £60 because he has only sold 400.

    If the newsagent buys 440 the cost is £66 but if he only sells 400 × 30p his profit is reduced to £120 − £66 = £54.

    So a pay off table would look like

Demand	Purchased per day			
	400	440	480	520
400	£60	£54	£48	£42
440	£60	£66	£54	£54
480	£60	£66	£72	£66
520	£60	£66	£72	£78

To calculate the expected value

Demand per day	Probability	Purchased per day			
		400	440	480	520
400	0.2	12	10.8	9.6	8.4
440	0.3	18	19.8	16.2	16.2
480	0.4	24	26.4	28.8	26.4
520	0.1	6	6.6	7.2	7.8
		60	63.60	61.8	58.8

Highest expected value 440 = £63.60
so B

8 Amount required = £50 winning number
         + £50 profit
         £100
No of tickets available = 40
so £2.50 each
so B

9 $\frac{35}{37} \times 100 = 95\%$

So on a £100 stake our rate of return is −5%
so A

10 The driver will pay a premium of £500 whether there is an accident or not
so expected value =
premium of   £500
less 1% of £20,000   (£200)
          £300

so C

Section C

Summarising and Analysing Data

Data Collection

Data Collection

7

❓ Concepts, definitions and short-form questions

1 Distinguish between data and information.

2 Explain the following terms

   (i)   random sampling
  (ii)   systematic sampling
 (iii) stratified sampling
 (iv) multi-stage sampling
  (v) cluster sampling
 (vi) quota sampling

3 What are the four main methods that primary data can be collected?

   (i)
  (ii)
 (iii)
 (iv)

4 Distinguish between primary and secondary data.

5 What are the four most important things to consider when constructing a frequency distribution?

   (i)
  (ii)
 (iii)
 (iv)

✓ Concepts, definitions and short-form solutions

1 *Data* consists of numbers, letters, symbols, facts, events and transactions which have been recorded but not yet processed into a form which is suitable for making decisions. *Information* is data which has been processed in such a way that it has meaning to the person who is receiving it.

2   *Sampling*

   (i)   A **random sample** is a sample taken in such a way that every member of the population has an equal chance of being selected.
   (ii) If the population is known and a sample size of a certain number is required then one in so many items is selected. This is **systematic sampling**.
   (iii) If the population being sampled contains several well defined groups (called strata) e.g. if 20% of the population are pensioners, this method of **stratified sampling** ensures that a representative cross section of the strata in the population is obtained.
   (iv) **Multi-stage sampling** would be used if you were carrying out a national survey e.g. an opinion poll prior to the election. The country would be divided into areas, then town or cities, then roads and streets, etc.
   (v)   **Cluster sampling** is similar to multi-stage sampling except that every house in a particular area would be visited rather than just a random sample.
   (vi) With **quota sampling** the person conducting the interview would be given a list or quota of certain individuals, for example, professional females aged 20–35 25%.

3   *Survey methods*

   (i)   postal questionnaire
   (ii) personal interview
   (iii) telephone interview
   (iv) observation

4   *Primary and secondary data*

   Primary data is data which has been specifically collected for a particular enquiry.
   Secondary data is data which has been collected for some other enquiry.

5   *Frequency distributions*

   The four most important things are

   (i)   number of classes
   (ii) class intervals or widths
   (iii) open ended class intervals
   (iv) class limits

❓ Multiple choice questions

1   Which of the following statements is correct?

   A   data + data   = information
   B   data + information   = meaning
   C   data + meaning   = information
   D   information + meaning = data

2   A sample taken in such a way that every member of the population has an equal chance of being selected is known as a

   A   random sample
   B   systematic sample
   C   stratified sample
   D   multi-stage sample

3   Stratified sampling is often preferred to systematic sampling because

   A   this method can be applied with the minimum of difficulty
   B   this method ensures that a representative cross section of the sample in the population is obtained
   C   it is carried out on a national basis
   D   there is no difference between stratified and systematic sampling

4   Which of the following methods can be used to collect primary data?

   (i)   postal questionnaire
   (ii)   personal interview
   (iii) telephone interview
   (iv)   observation

   A   i, ii
   B   i, ii, iv
   C   i, iii, iv
   D   i, ii, iii, iv

5   A management accountant is checking invoices for errors. Every invoice has a serial number the first being 3001. She has decided to sample 1 in 5 invoices. After selecting a random number from 1 to 5 she will then check invoices numbered 3005, 3010, 3020, etc. This sampling method is termed

   A   random
   B   stratified
   C   clustered
   D   systematic

? Multiple choice solutions

1   The statement which is correct is data + meaning = information.
   so C

2   A sample taken in such a way that every member of the population has an equal chance of being selected is known as a random sample.
   so A

3   Stratified sampling is often preferred to systematic sampling because this method ensures that a representative cross section of the sample in the population is obtained.
   so B

4   Postal questionnaires, personal interviews, telephone interviews and observation are all used to collect primary data.
   so D

5   This is an example of systematic sampling.
   so D

8

Presentation of Data

Presentation of Data

8

1 In constructing graphs and diagrams, state six principles which should be followed.

   (i)
   (ii)
   (iii)
   (iv)
   (v)
   (vi)

2 State three types of bar charts.

   (i)
   (ii)
   (iii)

3 A farmer has land extending to 100 acres which comprises 43% wheat, 20% barley, 16% grass, 12% oats and 9% fallow. If these figures were drawn in a pie chart what would be the angle of each?

4 United won the league last season using 20 players. There were 40 league games.

Players who played	Frequency
35–40 games	1
30–34 games	3
25–29 games	4
20–24 games	5
15–19 games	1
10–14 games	2
less than 10 games	4

Construct a frequency distribution showing the number of times players played.

5   Write down the values of the following.

    (i)   lower quartiles
   (ii)   upper quartiles
  (iii)   decile
  (iv)   percentile
   (v)   2nd decile

6   There are 100 packets of biscuits in a box with the following weights and frequencies

Weights	Frequency
100 and less than 110	1
110 and less than 120	2
120 and less than 130	5
130 and less than 140	11
140 and less than 150	21
150 and less than 160	20
160 and less than 170	17
170 and less than 180	11
180 and less than 190	6
190 and less than 200	6

Draw a cumulative frequency curve.

7   The following data was extracted from the annual report of XY plc.

	Annual sales (£millions)	
	2001	2002
UK	31.5	35.0
EC	33.2	47.4
USA	40.3	78.9
Australia	26.1	18.2
	131.1	179.5

Show this information

   (i)   in a pie chart
  (ii)   a component bar chart.

? Questions 8–10 are based on the following data

Student marks (%)	Number of students
Over 80	2
70–79	8
60–69	15
50–59	30
40–49	25
30–39	10
20–29	10
	100

8   From the information above construct a histogram.

9   From the information above construct a frequency polygon.

10   From the information above construct an ogive.

✓ Concepts, definitions and short-form solutions

1   Principles to be followed constructing graphs and diagrams

   (i)   give the diagram a name
   (ii)   state where data is sourced
   (iii) units of measurement must be stated
   (iv)   scale must be stated
   (v)   axes must be clearly labelled
   (vi)   neatness is essential

2   (i)   simple
   (ii)   component
   (iii) multiple

3   (i)   wheat $\dfrac{43}{100} \times 360$ 155°

   (ii)   barley $\dfrac{20}{100} \times 360$ 72°

   (iii) grass $\dfrac{16}{100} \times 360$ 58°

   (iv)   oats $\dfrac{12}{100} \times 360$ 43°

   (v)   fallow $\dfrac{9}{100} \times 360$ $\dfrac{72°}{360°}$

4

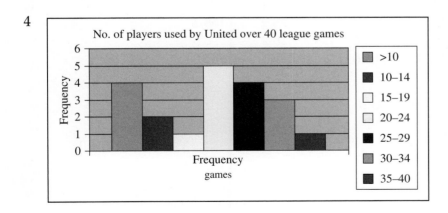

5   (i)   25% through the cumulative frequencies
   (ii)   75% through the cumulative frequencies
   (iii) 10% of the population
   (iv)   1% of the population
   (v)   20% through the cumulative frequencies

6

Class interval *Weight*	Frequency *No. of articles*	Cumulative *Frequency*
100 and less than 110	1	1
110 and less than 120	2	3
120 and less than 130	5	8
130 and less than 140	11	19
140 and less than 150	21	40
150 and less than 160	20	60
160 and less than 170	17	77
170 and less than 180	11	80
180 and less than 190	6	94
190 and less than 200	6	100

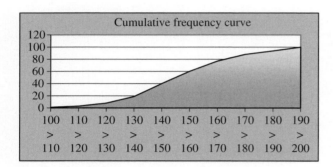

Note: Cumulative frequency is always plotted at the upper mathematical class limit.

7   (i)   Pie chart

	2001		2002	
	Sales	*Angles*	*Sales*	*Angles*
UK	31.5	86.5	35.0	70.2
EC	33.2	91.2	47.4	95.1
USA	40.3	110.7	78.9	158.2
Australia	26.1	71.6	18.2	36.5
	131.1	360.0	179.5	360.0

Radii of circles

$$= \sqrt{131.1} \quad \text{and} \quad \sqrt{179.5}$$
$$= 11.4 \quad \text{and} \quad 13.4$$

So if radius for 2001 = 3 cm

Radius for 2002 $= \dfrac{13.4}{11.4} \times 3 = 3.5$ cm

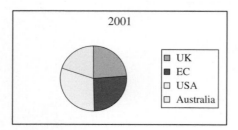

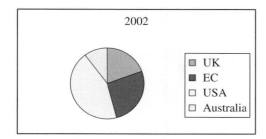

(ii)

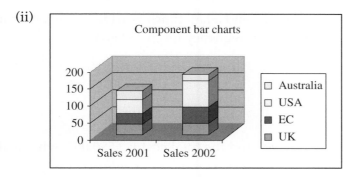

8

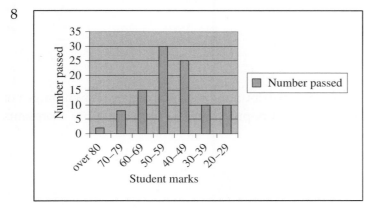

9

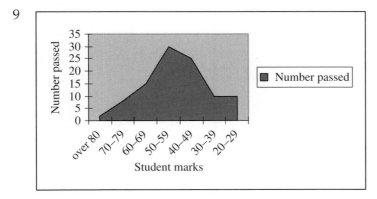

10

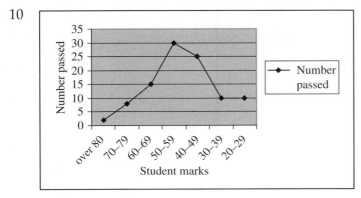

? Multiple choice questions

1 The difference in value between the lower quartile and the second decile is:

   A 5%
   B 10%
   C 20%
   D 25%

2 In a histogram in which one class interval is one and a half times as wide as the remaining classes, the height to be plotted in relation to the frequency for that class is

   A × 0.67
   B × 0.75
   C × 1
   D × 1.5

3 In a pie chart, if wages are represented by 90° and the total cost is £550,000, what is the amount paid out in wages?

   A £135,000
   B £137,500
   C £142,000
   D £145,000

4 An ogive represents a cumulative frequency distribution on which can be shown ranges of values containing given proportions of the total population. The upper quartile represents

   A 25% through the cumulative frequencies
   B 75% through the cumulative frequencies
   C 1% of the population
   D 10% of the population

5 The decile represents

   A 1% of the population
   B 10% of the population
   C the majority of the population
   D 90% of the population

6 Cumulative frequencies are plotted against

   A the mid-point
   B the lower class boundaries
   C the upper class boundaries
   D any of the above

7 A frequency distribution of a sample of monthly incomes is as follows

£	Frequency
400 and less than 800	7
800 and less than 1,000	16
1,000 and less than 1,200	28
1,200 and less than 1,300	21
1,300 and less than 1,400	8
	80

If the area between £800 and £1,000 has a height of 8 cm, what is the height of the rectangle 1,000 and less than 1,200?

A 10
B 12
C 14
D 16

8 The top 1% of the population is referred to statistically as

A percentile
B decile
C quartile
D 2nd decile

9 Which of the following are types of bar chart?

 (i) simple
(ii) multiple
(iii) component
(iv) compound

A i and ii
B i, ii, iv
C i, ii, iii
D i, ii, iii, iv

10 A histogram uses a set of rectangles to represent a grouped frequency table. To be correctly presented, the histogram must show the relationship of the rectangles to the frequencies by reference to the

A height of each rectangle
B area of each rectangle
C width of each rectangle
D diagonal of each rectangle

✓ Multiple choice solutions

1 Lower quartile is 25% through the cumulative frequencies, second decile is 20% through the cumulative frequencies.
So 5% - A.

2 The number of classes is small so odd one out is
D

Since we have multiplied one side by 1.5 we need to divide the other by 1.5 so 0.67.
so A

3 There are 360 degrees in a circle
so $\dfrac{90}{360} \times £550,000 = £137,500$
so B

4 The upper quartile represents 75% through the cumulative frequencies.
   so B

5 The decile represents 10% of the population.
   so B

6 Cumulative frequencies are plotted against the upper class boundaries.
   so C

7 Scale = 1 cm for 2 frequencies, then 28 should have a height of 14.
   so C

8 The top 1% of the population is referred to statistically as the percentile.
   so A

9 Simple, multiple, component and compound are all types of bar charts.
   so D

10 To be correctly presented, the histogram must show the relationship of the rectangles to the frequencies by reference to the area.
   so B

Averages

Averages

9

? Concepts, definitions and short-form questions

1 Distinguish between

   (i)   the mean
   (ii) the median
   (iii) the mode

2 State three advantages and two disadvantages of using the mean

   Advantages   *Disadvantages*
   (i)   (i)
   (ii)   (ii)
   (iii)

3 Calculate the arithmetic mean of 3, 6, 7, 8, 9, 11, 13, 15.

4 State four advantages and three disadvantages of using the median

   Advantages   *Disadvantages*
   (i)   (i)
   (ii)   (ii)
   (iii)   (iii)
   (iv)

5 Calculate the median of 3, 6, 10, 14, 17, 19 and 22.

6 State four advantages and three disadvantages of using the mode

   Advantages   *Disadvantages*
   (i)   (i)
   (ii)   (ii)
   (iii)   (iii)
   (iv)

7 In one over a batsman scored 4, 4, 2, 1, 0 and 4. Calculate the mode.

8   In his last two 72 hole competitions, a golfer scored 67, 71, 72, 73, 72, 69, 71, 72. Calculate

    (i)   his mean score
    (ii) his median score
    (iii) his mode score

9   How can the mode be determined from a histogram?

10 There are 100 packets of biscuits in a box with the following weights and frequencies

Weights	Frequency
100 and less than 110	1
110 and less than 120	2
120 and less than 130	5
130 and less than 140	11
140 and less than 150	21
150 and less than 160	20
160 and less than 170	17
170 and less than 180	11
180 and less than 190	6
190 and less than 200	6

What is the mean weight?

✓ Concepts, definitions and short-form solutions

1   (i)   The *arithmetic mean* is calculated by taking the total value of all items divided by the total number of items.
    (ii) The *median* is the value of the middle item in a distribution once all the items have been arranged in order of magnitude.
    (iii) The *mode* is the value that occurs most frequently amongst all the items in the distribution.

2   **The mean**

Advantages
    (i)   Easy to calculate and understand.
    (ii) All the data in the distribution is used.
    (iii) It can be used in more advanced mathematical statistics.

Disadvantages
    (i)   It may give undue weight or be influenced by extreme values e.g. income
    (ii) The value of the average may not correspond to any individual value in the distribution for example 2.2 children.

3   $\dfrac{3 + 6 + 7 + 8 + 9 + 11 + 13 + 15}{8} = \dfrac{72}{8} = 9$

4   **The median**

Advantages
    (i)   It is not affected by extreme values.
    (ii) It is easy to understand.

(iii) It is unaffected by unequal class intervals.

(iv) It can be the value of an actual item in the distribution.

Disadvantages

(i) If there are only a few items it can be unrepresentative.

(ii) It is unsuitable for use in mathematical tables.

(iii) Data has to be arranged in order of size which is time consuming.

5 Since there are three numbers below 14 and three numbers above 14, median is equal to 14.

6 **The mode**

Advantages

(i) It is easy to understand and calculate.

(ii) It is not affected by extreme values.

(iii) It can be calculated even if all the values in the distribution are not known.

(iv) It can be the value of an item in the distribution.

Disadvantages

(i) There may be no modal value or more than one may exist.

(ii) It is not suitable for mathematical statistics.

(iii) Data has to be arranged to ascertain which figure appears the most often.

7 The modal value is four since it appears three times.

8 Golfer's score

(i) Mean $= \dfrac{67 + 71 + 72 + 73 + 72 + 69 + 71 + 72}{8}$

   $= 71$

(ii) Median $= 67, 69, 71, 71, 72, 72, 72, 73$

   In this example the median is found by taking the arithmetic mean of 71 and 72 so 71.5

(iii) The score which appears the most frequently is 72.

9 **Estimation of mode for grouped data**

In a grouped frequency distribution, the modal class is the class with the largest frequency. This can easily be found by observation. The value of the mode within the modal class can then be estimated from a histogram.

Having located the modal class it is necessary to draw in the dotted lines shown in the following diagram.

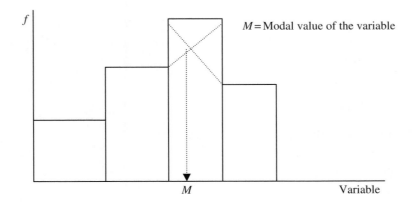

10

Class interval	Mid-value	Frequency	
Weight (grams)	*x*	*f*	*fx*
100 and less than 110	105	1	105
110 and less than 120	115	2	230
120 and less than 130	125	5	625
130 and less than 140	135	11	1,485
140 and less than 150	145	21	3,045
150 and less than 160	155	20	3,100
160 and less than 170	165	17	2,805
170 and less than 180	175	11	1,925
180 and less than 190	185	6	1,110
190 and less than 200	195	6	1,170
Total		$\Sigma f = 100$	$\Sigma fx = 15,600$

$$\overline{X} = \frac{\Sigma fx}{\Sigma f} = \frac{15,600}{100} = 156\,\text{g}$$

? Multiple choice questions

1 The arithmetic mean of 3, 6, 10, 14, 17, 19 and 22 is

A 11
B 13
C 14
D 15

2 The median of 3, 6, 10, 14, 17, 19 and 22 is

A 11
B 13
C 14
D 15

3 The mean weight of 10 parcels is 20 kg. If the individual weights in kilograms are 15, *x*, 22, 14, 21, 15, 20, *x*, 18, 27 then the value of *x* is

A 20 kg
B 24 kg
C 40 kg
D 48 kg

4 The mode is the value

A which appears with the highest frequency
B which is the same as the arithmetic mean
C which is the mid-point value
D none of the above

5 A factory employs staff in four departments for which the average mean wage per employee per week is as follows

Department	W	X	Y	Z
Mean wage	£50	£100	£70	£80
No. of employees	20	5	10	5

The average mean wage per employee is

A £60
B £65
C £70
D £75

6 If there are n items in the distribution the value of the median is

A $\dfrac{n + 1}{2}$

B $\dfrac{n - 1}{2}$

C $n + 1$
D $n - 1$

? **Questions 7–9 are based on the following data**

A sample of 12 packets of crisps taken from a box had the following weights in grams 504, 506, 501, 505, 507, 506, 504, 508, 503, 505, 502, 504.

7 Calculate the mean weight.

A 502.3
B 503.4
C 504.6
D 505.7

8 Calculate the median weight.

A 504
B 504.5
C 505
D 505.5

9 Calculate the modal weight.

A 504
B 505
C 506
D 507

10 Which of the following is **not** an advantage of the median?

A It is simple to understand
B It is not affected by extreme values
C It can be the value of an actual item in the distribution
D It is suitable for use in mathematical statistics

✓ Multiple choice solutions

1 Arithmetic mean $= \dfrac{3 + 6 + 10 + 14 + 17 + 19 + 22}{7}$

$= \dfrac{91}{7} = 13$

so B

2 Median is the value of the middle item. So there are three numbers below 14 and three numbers above.

so C

3 Mean $= 20 \text{ kg}$
Samples size $= 10$
so $15 + x + 22 + 14 + 21 + 15 + 20 + x + 18 + 27 = 200$
so $152 + 2x = 200$

$2x = 48$

$x = 24$

so B

4 The mode is the value which appears with the highest frequency.

so A

5

Dept.	Mean wage	No. of employees	Total
W	50	20	1,000
X	100	5	500
Y	70	10	700
Z	80	5	400
		40	2,600

Mean wage per employee $= \dfrac{£2,600}{40} = £65$

so B

6 If there are n items in the distribution the value of the median is $\dfrac{n + 1}{2}$.

so A

7 To make calculation easier subtract 500

so $500 \times \dfrac{4 + 6 + 1 + 5 + 7 + 6 + 4 + 8 + 3 + 5 + 2 + 4}{12}$

$= 500 \times \dfrac{55}{12} = 504.6$

so C

8 Arranging in numerical order we have
501, 502, 503, 504, 504, 504, 505, 505, 506, 506, 507, 508

Median $= \dfrac{504 + 505}{2} = 504.5$

so B

9 It is 504 since it appears three times.

so A

10 The median is not suitable for mathematical statistics.

so D

Variation

Variation

10

? Concepts, definitions and short-form questions

1 Calculate the standard deviation of 3, 4, 6, 8, 9.

2 In last Saturday's football matches there were 40 games played and the information below shows the number of bookings.

Number of bookings	Frequency
1	3
2	5
3	12
4	14
5	6

Calculate the standard deviation.

3 Given the following data on Product A and Product B, what is the coefficient of variation for each product?

	Mean	Standard deviation
Product A	5.46	1.29
Product B	16.38	4.21

4 What is the relationship between the mean, median and mode in

   (i)   a normal distribution
   (ii) a positively skewed distribution
   (iii) a negatively skewed distribution

5 If the mean is equal to 40 and the median is 37 and the standard deviation is equal to 9, calculate Pearson's coefficient of skewness.

6 The value of sales in Jimmy Farish's shop was

January	8,000	July	6,200
February	7,500	August	8,100
March	8,200	September	8,200
April	9,100	October	8,100
May	8,500	November	8,400
June	8,400	December	10,000

From this data calculate the standard deviation.

? ## Questions 7–10 are based on the following data

The numbers in seconds show the lap times of 40 drivers.

126	120	122	105	129	119	131	138
125	127	113	112	130	122	134	136
128	126	117	114	120	123	127	140
124	127	114	111	116	131	128	137
127	122	106	121	116	135	142	130

7 Group the data into eight classes.

8 Calculate

    (i)   the median value
   (ii) quartile value
  (iii) semi-inter quartile range

9 Calculate the mean of this frequency distribution.

10 Calculate the standard deviation.

✓ ## Concepts, definitions and short-form solutions

1   x x^2

x	x^2
3	9
4	16
6	36
8	64
9	81
30	206

$$\delta = \sqrt{\frac{206}{5} - \left(\frac{30}{5}\right)^2}$$
$$= \sqrt{41.2 - 36}$$
$$= \sqrt{5.2}$$
$$= 2.28$$

2   x

x	Frequency	fx	fx^2
1	3	3	3
2	5	10	20
3	12	36	108
4	14	56	224
5	6	30	300
Total	40	135	655

$$\delta = \sqrt{\frac{655}{40} - \left(\frac{135}{40}\right)^2}$$
$$= \sqrt{16.38 - 11.42}$$
$$= \sqrt{4.96}$$
$$= 2.22$$

3 Product A coefficient of variation $= \dfrac{1.29 \times 100}{5.46} = 23.63\%$

   Product B coefficient of variation $= \dfrac{4.21 \times 100}{16.38} = 25.7\%$

4 (i)   They all have the same value.
   (ii) Mean highest, median middle and mode lowest value.
   (iii) Mean lowest, median middle and mode highest value.

5 Pearson's coefficient of skewness $= \dfrac{3(\text{mean} - \text{median})}{\text{Standard deviation}}$

$$= \dfrac{3 \times (40 - 37)}{9}$$

$$= \dfrac{9}{9}$$

$$= 1$$

6

x	x^2
8,000	64,000
7,500	56,250
8,200	67,240
9,100	82,810
8,500	72,250
8,400	70,560
6,200	38,440
8,100	65,610
8,200	67,240
8,100	65,610
8,400	70,560
10,000	100,000
98,700	820,570

$$\delta = \sqrt{\dfrac{820{,}570}{12} - \left(\dfrac{98{,}700}{12}\right)^2}$$

$$= \sqrt{68{,}380.83 - 67{,}650.63 - 36}$$

$$= \sqrt{730.20}$$

$$= 27.02$$

7

Time	Tally	Frequency
105 > 110	II	2
110 > 115		5
115 > 120	IIII	4
120 > 125	III	8
125 > 130		10
130 > 135		5
135 > 140	IIII	4
140 > 145	II	2

8 By constructing cumulative frequency distribution

    (i)   median   = 125 seconds

    (ii)   1st quartile   = 119 seconds

          3rd quartile   = 131 seconds

    (iii)   semi inter quartile range $= \dfrac{1}{2}(131 - 119)$

                                          = 6 seconds

9

Time	Mid-point	F	fx	fx²
105–110	107.5	2	215	23,112.50
110–115	112.5	5	562.5	63,281.25
115–120	117.5	4	470	55,225.00
120–125	122.5	8	980	120,050.00
125–130	127.5	10	1,275	162,562.50
130–135	132.5	5	662.5	87,781.25
135–140	137.5	4	550	75,625.00
140–145	142.5	2	285	40,612.50
		$\Sigma f = 40$	$\Sigma fx = 5{,}000$	$\Sigma fx^2 = 628{,}250.00$

$$\text{Mean} = \frac{\Sigma fx}{\Sigma f} = \frac{5{,}000}{40} = 125 \text{ seconds}$$

10 Standard deviation $= \sqrt{\dfrac{628{,}250}{40} - \left(\dfrac{5{,}000}{40}\right)^2}$

                                   $= 9.01\%$

? Multiple choice questions

1 The following data relate to a frequency distribution

mean 34   median 32   standard deviation 12

Pearson's coefficient of skewness is equal to

A   3

B   2

C   1

D   0.5

2 Several groups of invoices are being analysed. For each group the coefficient of variation has been calculated. The coefficient of variation measures

A   the range of values between the invoices

B   the correlation between the invoice values

C   the relative dispersion of the invoice values

D   the variation between the sample mean and the true mean

3 The standard deviation of 3, 5, 8, 11 and 13 is

A   3.69

B   4.25

C   5.41
D   7.62

4   In a negatively skewed distribution, which of the above statements are true?

   (i)   the mean is below the median
   (ii)   the mean is below the mode
   (iii)   the median is above the mean
   (iv)   the median is above the mode

A   i, ii
B   i, ii, iii
C   i, ii, iv
D   i, ii, iii, iv

5   If the standard deviation is 1.1 and the arithmetic mean is 3.5 then the coefficient of variation is equal to

A   29.86
B   31.43
C   33.79
D   34.61

6   The interval between the upper quarter and the lower quarter is known as

A   the mean
B   the standard deviation
C   the mode
D   the inter quartile range

7   Four products have the same mean weight of 250 grams but their standard deviates are

Product A   10 grams
Product B   15 grams
Product C   20 grams
Product D   25 grams

Which product has the highest coefficient of variation?

A   Product A
B   Product B
C   Product C
D   Product D

8   Which of the following are advantages of the semi-inter quartile range?

   (i)   it is simple to understand
   (ii)   it is not affected by extreme values
   (iii)   it takes all values into account
   (iv)   it can be used in mathematical statistics

A   i, ii
B   ii, iii
C   i, iv
D   iii, iv

9 In a negatively skewed distribution the peak will be closest to

    A   the mean
    B   the mode
    C   the median
    D   none of the above

✓ Multiple choice solutions

1   Pearson's coefficient of skewness $= \dfrac{3(\text{mean} - \text{median})}{\text{Standard deviation}}$

$$= \frac{3(34 - 32)}{12}$$

$$= 0.5$$

   so D

2   The coefficient of variation measures the relative dispersion of the given data.
   so C

3

x	x^2
3	9
5	25
8	64
11	121
13	169
$\Sigma 40$	$\Sigma x^2 = 388$

$$r = \frac{\sqrt{388 - (40)^2}}{\sqrt{5 - (5)^2}}$$

$$= \sqrt{77.6 - 64}$$

$$= \sqrt{13.6}$$

$$= 3.69$$

   so A

4   In a negatively skewed distribution the mean is below the median, the mean is below the mode, and the median is above the mean.
   so B
   A negatively skewed distribution

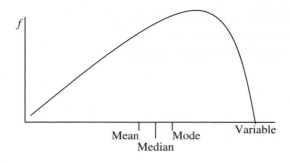

5 Coefficient of variation $= \dfrac{\text{Standard deviation} \times 100}{\text{Arithmetic mean}}$

$$= \frac{110}{3.5} = 31.43$$

so B

6 The interval between the upper quarter and the lower quarter is known as the inter quartile range.
so D

7 Product A $\dfrac{10}{250} \times 100 = 4$

   Product B $\dfrac{15}{250} \times 100 = 6$

   Product C $\dfrac{20}{200} \times 100 = 8$

   Product D $\dfrac{25}{250} \times 100 = 10$

so highest is Product D,
so D

8 The only advantages are

   (i)   it is simple to understand and
   (ii) it is not affected by extreme values

   so A

9 A distribution will peak at the mode whether it is normal, positive or negative since it is the value which occurs the most frequently,
so B

The Normal Distribution

The Normal Distribution

11

? **Concepts, definitions and short-form questions**

1   State five features of a normal distribution curve.

   (i)
   (ii)
   (iii)
   (iv)
   (v)

2   Give three examples where a normal distribution might appear in real life.

   (i)
   (ii)
   (iii)

3   A group of workers have a weekly wage which is normally distributed with a mean of £400 and a standard deviation of £60. What is the probability of a worker earning.

   (i)   more than £430
   (ii)   less than £350
   (iii) more than £460
   (iv)   between £350 and £430
   (v)   between £430 and £460?

4   *Confidence limits*

   (i)   There is a 95% probability that the population mean lies within $+/-$ .... standard errors of a sample mean.
   (ii) There is a 98% probability that the population mean lies within $+/-$ .... standard errors of a sample mean.
   (iii) There is a 99% probability that the population mean lies within $+/-$ .... standard errors of a sample mean.

5   The Island of Dreams has a temperature which is normally distributed with a mean of 70° and a standard deviation of 5°. What is the probability of

   A   (i)   the temperature below 60°
       (ii)   no lower than 65°
       (iii) higher than 85°
       (iv)   between 67° and 74°
   B   What is the maximum temperature that has no more than a 1% chance of being exceeded?

6   The mean weight of a bag of crisps is 50 g and a standard deviation of 10 g. What is the probability that a sample of 100 packets will have a mean of less than 48 g?

✓ Concepts, definitions and short-form solutions

1   (i)   It is symmetrical and bell shaped.
    (ii) Both tails approach but never reach the X axis.
    (iii) The mean, median and mode are equal.
    (iv) The area under the curve is equal to 1 and the areas left and right of the mean are equal to 0.5 each.
    (v)   It is a mathematical curve which closely fits many natural occurring distributions.

2   (i)   heights of people
    (ii) weights of people
    (iii) examination marks

3   (i) $\dfrac{430 - 400}{60} = 0.5$
          from table area above 430 is 0.3085 or approximately 31%.

    (ii) $\dfrac{350 - 400}{60} = -0.83$
          from table area below 350 is 0.2033 or approximately 20%.

    (iii) $\dfrac{460 - 400}{60} = 1$
          from table area above 460 = 0.1587 or approximately 16%.

    (iv) Area less than £350 has already been found in (ii) = 0.2033
          therefore area between £350 and £400 = 0.5 − 0.2033 = 0.2967
          similarly area over £430 has already been found in (i) = 0.3085
          therefore area between £400 and £430 = 0.5 − 0.3085 = 0.1915
          therefore area between £350 and £430 = 0.2967 + 0.1915 = 0.4882
          so approximately 49% earn between £350 and £430.

    (v)   If area over £430 is 0.3085 then area between £400 and £430 is 0.5 − 0.3085 = 0.1915
          If area over £460 is 0.1587 then area between £400 and £460 is 0.5 − 0.1587 = 0.3413
          so area between £430 and £460 = 0.3413 − 0.1915 = 0.1498
          so approximately 15% earn between £430 and £460.

4   (i)   1.96
    (ii) 2.33
    (iii) 2.58

5   A   (i) $Z = \dfrac{x - v}{\sigma} \dfrac{60 - 70}{5} = -\dfrac{10}{5} = -2$
              from tables 0.02275
              Thus the chance of temperature being below 60° is 2.2%.

        (ii) $Z = \dfrac{65 - 70}{5} = 1$

              from tables probability of temperature less than 65° is 0.1587.
              So probability that temperature is no lower than 65%
              = 1 − 0.1587 = 0.8413
              So there is an 84% chance temperature is no lower than 65°.

        (iii) $Z = \dfrac{85 - 70}{5} = 3$

B   Since most normal distribution tables only go up to 2.99
    we cannot find value of 3.
    However, taking a guess it would be about 1%.

6   $u = 50$
    $\sigma = 10$
    $n = 100$
    $x = 48$

Standard error $= \dfrac{\sigma}{n} = \dfrac{10}{100} = 0.1$

$$Z = \dfrac{48 - 50}{1} = -2$$

from table area $= 0.2275$
that is 48 is Z standard errors below mean weight of 50
so probability $= 22.75\%$.

? Multiple choice questions

Questions 1–7 are based on the following information

A group of workers have a weekly wage which is normally distributed with a mean of £360 per week and a standard deviation of £15.

1   What is the probability a worker earns more than £380?

   A   4%
   B   5%
   C   7%
   D   9%

2   What is the probability a worker earns less than £330?

   A   1%
   B   2%
   C   3%
   D   4%

3   What is the probability a worker earns more than £420?

   A   5%
   B   4%
   C   2%
   D   0%

4   What is the probability a worker earns between £330 and £390?

   A   50%
   B   75%
   C   90%
   D   95%

5   What is the probability a worker earns between £370 and £400?

    A   1%
    B   15%
    C   20%
    D   25%

6   What are the limits which enclose the middle 98%?

    A   £330.60 and £389.40
    B   £325.05 and £394.95
    C   £320.40 and £400.40
    D   £300 and £450

7   A normal distribution has a mean of 75 and a variance of 25. The upper quartile of this distribution is
    A   58.25
    B   71.65
    C   78.35
    D   91.75

8   A normal distribution has a mean of 150 and a standard deviation of 20. Eighty per cent of this distribution is below
    A   150
    B   154.8
    C   159.6
    D   166.8

9   In a normal distribution with a mean of 150, 6.68% of the population is above 180. The standard deviation of the distribution is
    A   10
    B   15
    C   20
    D   25

10 Which of the following is not a feature of a normal distribution?
    A   It is symmetrical
    B   It is bell-shaped
    C   The mean is equal to the mode
    D   The mean is above the median

✓ Multiple choice solutions

1   $Z = \dfrac{380 - 360}{15} = 1.33$

From normal distribution table
$Z = 0.4082$
So probability $> Z = 0.5 - 0.4082$
$$= 0.0918$$
$$= 9\%$$

so D

2 $Z = \dfrac{330 - 360}{15} = -2$

From normal distribution table

$Z = 0.4772$

So probability $Z < £330 = 0.5 - 0.4772$
$$= 0.0228$$
$$= 2\%$$

so B

3 $Z = \dfrac{420 - 360}{15} = 4$

Highest value in the normal distribution table is 3.5, so it is impossible for worker to earn more than £420 from the data so no chance 0%.

so D

4 Area between 330 and 360 = 0.4772 from Question 2.

$\dfrac{390 - 360}{15} = 2$ is also 0.4772

so 0.4722 + 0.4722 = 0.9544 so approximately 95%.

so D

5 Required area is between 370 and 400

$\dfrac{400 - 360}{15} = 2.666 = 0.4962$

$\dfrac{370 - 360}{15} = 0.67 = 0.2486$

so 0.4962 − 0.2486 = 0.2476 or approximately 25%.

so D

6 For an area of 0.49 $Z = 2.33$

$$\dfrac{x - 360}{15} = \pm 2.33$$

£360 + (£15 × 2.33) = £394.95
£360 − (£15 × 2.33) = £325.05

Middle 98% lies between £325.05 and £394.95.

so B

7 The area under the normal curve we require the Z factor to be 0.25.

Combined with the area below the mean, this will give a total value of 0.75 that is, the upper quartile

Nearest value to 0.25 = 0.2486 = 0.67

So 0.67 × standard deviation $\sqrt{25} = 5$

We get 3.35. The upper quartile is 3.35 above the mean of 75 so 78.35.

so C

8   From the normal distribution table, 30% of a distribution lies between the mean and 0.84 standard deviation above the mean

so $x = 150 + (0.84 \times 20)$

$\quad = 166.8$

so D

9   If 6.68% of the population is above 180, then $0.5 - 0.0668 = 0.4332$

so $Z = 1.5$

so $Z = \dfrac{x^1 - u}{u} = 1.5$

$1.5 = 180 - 150$

$u = \dfrac{30}{1.5}$

$\quad = 20$

so C

10 Odd-one-out is D since, in a normal distribution, the mean is equal to the mode which is equal to the median.

Section D

Interrelationship between variables

12

Statistical Inference

Statistical
Inference

12

1   95% confidence limits $= \bar{x} \pm$ .... standard errors
    98% confidence limits $= \bar{x} \pm$ .... standard errors
    99% confidence limits $= \bar{x} \pm$ .... standard errors

2   In a sample of 100 students, their mean height was 168.75 cm and the standard deviation was 7.5 cm. Find the 95% confidence intervals.

3   A sample of 100 items in a production line had a mean weight of 8.4 kg with a standard deviation of 0.5 kg. What is the 95% confidence interval for the mean weight of all items on the production line?

4   Past experience shows that 50% of students pass Business Mathematics at the first attempt. What is the probability that 55% or more of a group of 200 students pass?

5   In a random sample of 100 voters 55% stated they would vote for candidate A. Calculate the 95% confidence limits for the proportion of all voters in favour of candidate A.

? **Questions 6, 7 and 8 are based on the following data**

A random sample of 100 candles was found to have a mean life of 360 hours with a standard deviation of 30 hours.

6   Calculate the standard error of the mean.

7   Calculate
    (i)   the 95% confidence intervals
    (ii) the 99% confidence intervals

8   The sample size necessary to provide a degree of accuracy within .... hours at the 95% level.

? **Questions 9 and 10 are based on the following information**

In a random sample of 400 of a direct mail CD club, the mean value per order was £30 with a standard deviation of £10. The average price per CD was £15.

105

9   Find 95% confidence limits for the mean and what does this indicate?

10 If the sample contains 80 teenagers, find 99% confidence interval for the population percentage of teenage customers.

✓ Concepts, definitions and short-form solutions

1   (i)   1.96
    (ii) 2.33
    (iii) 2.58

2   95% confidence interval $= 168.75 \pm 1.96 \times \dfrac{7.5}{\sqrt{100}}$

$$= 168.75 \pm 1.96 \times 0.75$$
$$= 168.75 \pm 1.47$$
$$= 167.28 - 170.22$$

3   95% confidence interval $= \bar{x} \pm 1.96\dfrac{\sigma}{\sqrt{n}}$

$$= 8.4 \pm 1.96 \times \dfrac{0.5}{\sqrt{100}}$$
$$= 8.4 \pm 1.96 \times 0.05$$
$$= 8.302 - 8.498$$

4   Population proportion $= 50\%$ or 0.5
    $p = 0.5 \qquad q = 1 - 0.5 \qquad n = 200$

$$\text{Standard error} = \sqrt{\dfrac{pq}{n}}$$
$$= \sqrt{\dfrac{0.5 \times 0.5}{200}}$$
$$= \sqrt{0.00125} = 0.03536$$

Standardising 0.55

$$z = \dfrac{0.55 - 0.5}{0.03536} = 1.41$$

From table $0.5 - 0.4207 = 0.0793$
Thus chances of 55% or more passing is approximately 8%.

5   $p = 0.55 \qquad q = 1 - 0.55 = 0.45 \qquad n = 100$

$$\text{So standard error} = \sqrt{\dfrac{pq}{n}}$$
$$= \sqrt{\dfrac{0.55 \times 0.45}{100}}$$
$$= 0.04975$$

95% confidence limits $= 0.55 \pm 1.96 \times 0.04975$
$$= 0.55 \pm 0.0975$$
$$= 0.45 - 0.65$$

This means there is a 95% probability that the proportion of all voters in favour of candidate A is between 45% and 65%.

6 Standard error $= \dfrac{\sigma}{\sqrt{n}} = \dfrac{30}{\sqrt{100}} = 3$ hours

7 (i) 95% confidence interval for $u = \bar{x} \pm 1.96\,\dfrac{\sigma}{\sqrt{n}}$

$$= 360 \pm 1.96 \times 3$$
$$= 360 \pm 5.88$$
$$= 354 \text{ hours} - 366 \text{ hours approx.}$$

 (ii) 99% confidence interval for $u = \bar{x} \pm 2.58 \times 3$
$$= 360 \pm 7.74$$

So $352.26 - 367.74 = 352 - 368$ hours to nearest hour

8 $1.96 \times \dfrac{\sigma}{\sqrt{n}} = 3$

$1.96 \times \dfrac{30}{\sqrt{n}} = 3$

$\dfrac{1.96 \times 30}{3} = \sqrt{n}$

$\sqrt{n} = 19.6$

$n = 384.16$

n must be at least 385

9 Standard error $= \dfrac{\sigma}{\sqrt{n}} = \dfrac{£10}{\sqrt{400}} = 50\text{p}$

95% confidence limits $= £30 \pm 1.96 \times 50\text{p}$
$$= £30 \pm 98\text{p}$$
$$= £29.02 \text{ and } £30.98$$

This means that there is a probability of 95% that the mean value of all orders lies between £29.02 and £30.98.

10 Standard error or proportion $= \sqrt{\dfrac{p(1-p)}{n}}$

$$p = \dfrac{80}{400} = 0.2$$

Standard error $= \sqrt{\dfrac{0.2 \times 0.8}{400}}$

$$= 0.02$$

99% confidence limits $=$ sample proportion ± 2.58 standard errors
$$= 0.2 \pm 2.58 \times 0.02$$
$$= 0.2 \pm 0.0516$$

This means that there is a 99% probability that the percentage of all customers who are teenagers is between 14.84% and 25.16%.

❓ Multiple choice questions

Questions 1–4 are based on the following information

A manufacturer of light bulbs needs to estimate the average burning life of each bulb he makes. From a random sample of 100 bulbs, it was found that they had a mean life of 340 hours with a standard deviation of 30 hours.

1   The standard error of mean was

   A   1 hour
   B   2 hours
   C   3 hours
   D   4 hours

2   The 95% confidence interval was

   A   334–346
   B   332–348
   C   330–350
   D   328–352

3   The 99% confidence interval was

   A   334–346
   B   332–348
   C   330–350
   D   328–352

4   The sample size necessary to provide a degree of accuracy within 3 hours at the 95% level was

   A   370
   B   375
   C   380
   D   385

? Questions 5 and 6 are based on the following data

A sample of 40 invoices are selected at random. The average value of the sample was £48.20 with a standard deviation of £7.40.

5   The 95% confidence limits for the average of all invoices is

   A   £45.91–£50.49
   B   £40.91–£55.49
   C   £35.91–£60.49
   D   £30.91–£65.49

6   How many invoices would need to be inspected for the average to be estimated to within £2 either side?

   A   51
   B   52
   C   53
   D   54

7   A sample size 100 has a mean of 120.87 and a variance of 81. The 95% upper confidence limit of the population mean is

   A   122.634
   B   123.162
   C   127.823
   D   136.746

8   A sample standard deviation tends to underestimate the population standard deviation. A better estimate is obtained by multiplying the sample standard deviation by $\dfrac{\sqrt{n}}{n-1}$.

This is known as

A   Bessels correction
B   Pearson's coefficient
C   Statistical inference
D   Point estimate of the parameter

9   A sample of 100 items on a production line has a mean weight of 8.4 g with a standard deviation of 0.5 g. What is the 95% confidence interval for the mean weight of all items on the production line?

A $8.302 < u < 8.498$
B $8.264 < u < 8.569$
C $8.154 < u < 8.623$
D $8.042 < u < 8.749$

10   In a random sample of 100 drives a golfer has a mean drive of 340 yards with a standard deviation of 30 yards. The standard error of the mean was

A   3 yards
B   30 yards
C   300 yards
D   impossible to determine

✓ Multiple choice solutions

1   Standard error $= \dfrac{\text{Standard deviation}}{\sqrt{n}}$

$= \dfrac{30}{\sqrt{100}} = 3$ hours

so C

2   95% confidence interval
$= \bar{x} \pm 1.96 \times \text{standard error}$
$= 340 \pm 1.96 \times 3$ hours
$= 340 \pm 5.88$
$= 334\text{–}346$

so A

3   99% confidence limit
$= 340 \pm 2.58 \times 3$
$= 340 \pm 7.74$ hours
$= 332\text{–}348$

so B

4   The error in the estimate $= 3$ hours

$1.96 \times \dfrac{\text{Standard deviation}}{\sqrt{n}} = 3$

$1.96 \times \dfrac{30}{\sqrt{n}} = 3$

$$\frac{1.96 \times 30}{3} = \sqrt{n}$$
$$19.6 = \sqrt{n}$$
$$n = 384.16$$

so n must be 385

so D

5   95% confidence interval $= 48.20 \pm 1.96 \times 1.171$
$$= 48.20 \pm 2.29$$

Thus we can be 95% confident that average invoices are between £45.91 and £50.49.

so A

6    $1.96 \times \dfrac{7.40}{\sqrt{n}} \leq 2$

Rearrange $1.96\,(7.40) \leq \sqrt{n}$
$$n \geq (7.252)^2 = 53$$

so C

7   The 95% confidence interval for the population mean is

$$\bar{x} \pm 1.96\,\frac{\sigma}{\sqrt{n}}$$

where $\bar{x}$ is the mean

σ is the standard deviation

n is the sample size

We are given a variance of 81, the standard deviation $= \sqrt{variance}$, so

Standard deviation $(\sigma) = \sqrt{81} = 9$

The given values and the calculated standard deviation need only be entered into the expression.

Hence $120.87 \pm 1.96\,\dfrac{(9)}{(\sqrt{100})}$
$$= 120.87 \pm 1.96(0.9)$$
$$= 120.87 \pm 1.764$$

The question asks for the upper confidence limit
$$= 120.87 + 1.764 = 122.634$$

so A

8   This is known as Bessels Correction

so A

9   95% confidence interval

$$= \bar{x} \pm 1.96\,\frac{\sigma}{\sqrt{n}}$$

$$= 8.4 \pm 1.96\,\frac{0.5}{\sqrt{100}\,\text{g}}$$
$$= 8.4 \pm 1.96 \times 0.05\,\text{g}$$
$$= 8.302 < u < 8.498$$

so A

10   Standard error of mean $= \dfrac{\sigma}{\sqrt{n}}$

$$= \frac{30}{\sqrt{100}} = 3 \text{ yards}$$

so A

13

Correlation
and Regression

Correlation and Regression

13

? Concepts, definitions and short-form questions

Questions 1 and 2 are based on the following

Records have been kept over eight quarters of the power costs of a central heating system and the hours used, as follows

Period	Hours used	Power costs
1	25	124
2	22	131
3	16	98
4	12	74
5	7	56
6	8	65
7	15	114
8	12	86

1 (a) Using the method of least squares, calculate the fixed elements of cost.
  (b) Calculate the variable elements of cost.

2 If the coefficient of determination is 0.87, what does this signify?

? Questions 3 and 4 are based on the following

Fertiliser (kg used)	*Yield* (tonnes)
100	40
200	45
300	50
400	65
500	70
600	70
700	80

3 Complete the regression line $y = ?$

4   Calculate the correlation coefficient.

5   The following table shows the ranking of six students in two tests.

Student	Maths test	English test
A	4	2
B	5	3
C	2	1
D	1	4
E	3	5
F	6	6

  (i)   what is the correlation coefficient?
 (ii)   Is there?
     (a) Positive correlation
     (b) Negative correlation
     (c) Little or no correlation

The correlation coefficient R, depicts the linear relationship between two variables.

6   (i)   for a perfect correlation $R =$
  (ii)   for a perfect negative correlation $R =$
 (iii)   for no correlation $R =$

7   A company's weekly costs £c were plotted against production levels (P) and a regression line calculated to be C = £1,000 + £7.5 g. Calculate the total cost if 5,000 units were produced.

8   Reject rates achieved by 100 factory operatives is to be found by the regression equation $y = 20 - 0.25x$ where $y = $ % of reject rates and x the months of experience. What would be the predicted reject rate for an operator with one year's experience?

❓ Questions 9 and 10 are based on the following data

You are asked to investigate the relationship between what a tyre company spend on rubber and their production. You are given information over the past ten months.

Month	1	2	3	4	5	6	7	8	9	10
Production X 000 units	30	20	10	60	40	25	13	50	44	28
Rubber costs Y £000	10	11	6	18	13	10	10	20	17	15

9   Complete the regression line $y = $.

10   If production is budgeted for 15,000 units and 55,000 units for the next two months, how much is likely to be spent on rubber?

✓ Concepts, definitions and short-form solutions

1

X	Y	XY	X^2
25	124	3,100	625
22	131	2,882	484
16	98	1,568	256
12	74	888	144
7	56	392	49
8	65	520	64
15	114	1,710	225
12	86	1,032	144
$\Sigma X = 117$	$\Sigma Y = 748$	$\Sigma XY = 12,092$	$\Sigma X^2 = 1,991$

$Y = a + bx$ where a = fixed costs and b = variable costs

$$b = \frac{(8 \times 12{,}092) - (117 \times 748)}{(8 \times 1{,}991) - (117 \times 117)}$$

$$= \frac{96{,}736 - 87{,}516}{15{,}928 - 13{,}689}$$

$$= \frac{9{,}220}{2{,}239}$$

$$= £4.12$$

$$a = \frac{748}{8} - 4.12 \times \frac{117}{8}$$

$$= 93.50 - 60.26$$

$$= £33.24$$

Fixed cost = £33.24
Variable cost = £4.12

2   A value of 0.87 indicates a high degree of positive correlation between hours used and power costs. This tells us that 87% of the variation in power costs can be attributed to changes in the hours used and 13% on other factors. However, a sample of eight is quite small. Nevertheless, +0.87 is close to +1 which indicates a perfect positive relationship.

✓ Solutions 3 and 4

X	Y	XY	X^2
1	40	40	1
2	45	90	4
3	50	150	9
4	65	260	16
5	70	350	25
6	70	420	36
7	80	560	49
28	420	1,870	140

3 $b = \dfrac{(7 \times 1,870) - (28 \times 420)}{(7 \times 140) - (28 \times 28)}$

$ = \dfrac{13,090 - 11,760}{980 - 784} = 6.79$

$a = \dfrac{420}{7} - 6.79 \times \dfrac{28}{7}$

$ = 60 - 27.16 = 32.84$

Regression line for y on $x = y = 32.84 + 6.79x$

4 $\dfrac{7 \times 1,870 - (28 \times 420)}{\sqrt{7 \times 140 - (28 \times 28)}\, 7 \times 26,550 - 420)^2}$

$= \dfrac{13,090 - 11,760}{\sqrt{(980 - 784)(185,850 - 176,400)}}$

$= \dfrac{1,330}{\sqrt{196 \times 9,450}}$

$= 0.98$

5 (i)

Student	Maths test	English test	D	D^2
A	4	2	2	4
B	5	3	2	4
C	2	1	1	1
D	1	4	−3	9
E	3	5	−2	4
F	6	6	0	0
			ΣD_0	ΣD^2

$r = 1 - \dfrac{6 \times 22}{6 \times (6^2 - 1)}$

$ = 1 - \dfrac{132}{210}$

$ = \dfrac{78}{210}$

$ = 0.37$

(ii) (c)

6 (i) +1

(ii) −1

(iii) 0

7 £1,000 + 5,000 (7.5 g)

 = £1,000 + £37,500

 = £38,500

8 $y = 20 - 0.25x$

If $x = 12$ $\quad y = 20 - 0.25 \times 12$

$ y = 20 - 3$

$ y = 17\%$

9 $\Sigma x = 320$
   $\Sigma y = 130$
   $n = 10$
   $\Sigma xy = 4{,}728$

$$b = \frac{10 \times 4{,}728(-320 \times 130)}{10 \times 12{,}614 - 320^2}$$

$$= \frac{5{,}680}{23{,}740}$$

$$= 0.239$$

$$a = \frac{130 - 0.239 \times 320}{10}$$

$$= 5.34$$

Least squares regression is $y = 5.34 + 0.239x$

10 $5.34 + 0.239 \times 15 = 8.93$ so £8,930
    $5.34 + 0.239 \times 55 = 18.5$ so £18,500

? Multiple choice questions

1 If $\Sigma x = 560$ $\Sigma y = 85$ $\Sigma x^2 = 62{,}500$
   $\Sigma xy = 14{,}200$ and $n = 12$, the regression line of y on x is equal to

   A $-0.281 + 6.03x$
   B $-6.03 + 0.281x$
   C $0.281 + 6.03x$
   D $6.03 + 0.281x$

2 In a forecasting model based on $y = a + bx$, the intercept is £234. If the value of y is £491 and $x = 20$ then b is equal to

   A 12.25
   B 12.85
   C 13.35
   D 13.95

3 A company's weekly costs £C were plotted against production levels for the last 50 weeks and a regression line C = 1,000 + 250p was found. This would denote that

   A fixed costs are £1,250
   B variable costs are £1,250
   C fixed costs are £1,000; variable costs £2.50
   D fixed costs are £250; variable costs are £1,000

4 The following table shows the ranking of six students in their CIMA Economics and CIMA Business Mathematics

Student	Economics rank	Maths rank
A	4	2
B	5	3
C	2	1
D	1	4
E	3	5
F	6	6

What is the correlation between the two subjects?

A 0.31
B 0.33
C 0.35
D 0.37

5 Management accountants require to calculate costs. The variable to be predicted is known as the

A dependent variable
B statistical variable
C independent variable
D high-low variable

6 What type of relationship would there likely be between the cost of electricity and electricity production levels?

A perfect positive linear
B perfect negative linear
C high positive
D low negative

7 The coefficient of determination (R^2) explains the

A percentage variation in the coefficient of correlation
B percentage variation in the dependent variable which is explained by the independent variable
C percentage variation in the independent variable which is explained by the dependent variable
D extent of the casual relationship between the two variables

8 In a forecast model based on $y = a + bx$, the interest is £234. If the value of y is £491 and x is 20 then the value of the slope =

A −24.55
B −12.85
C 12.85
D 24.85

9   In the equation $y = a + bx$, a is equal to

    A   the intercept
    B   the gradient
    C   the regression line
    D   the coefficient

10   If there is a perfect positive correlation between two variables then the value of R, the correlation coefficient is

    A   greater than 1
    B   equal to 1
    C   equal to 0
    D   equal to -1

✅ Multiple choice solutions

1   Equation of line is $y = a + bx$

$$b = \frac{(12 \times 14{,}200) - (560 \times 85)}{12 \times 62{,}500 - 560 \times 560} = \frac{122{,}800}{436{,}400}$$

$b = 0.281$

$$a = \frac{85}{12} - 0.281 \times \frac{560}{12} = -6.03$$

Regression line is $y = -6.03 + 0.281x$
so B

2   $491 = 234 + 20b$

$$b = \frac{491 - 234}{20} = 12.85$$

so B

3   Fixed costs are £1,000; variable costs are £2.50
so C

4
Student	Economics	Maths	D	D^2
A	4	2	2	4
B	5	3	2	4
C	2	1	1	1
D	1	4	-3	9
E	3	5	-2	4
F	6	6	0	0
				22

$1 - 6(2^2) = 1 - 132$
$6(36 - 1) = 210$
          $= 1 - 0.63$
          $= 0.37$

so D

5 The variable to be predicted depends on some other variable
so A

6 Perfect positive linear, that is, rise by a constant amount
so A

7 The coefficient of determination (R^2) explains the percentage variation in the dependent variable which is explained by the independent variable.
so B

8 $Y = a + bx$
$491 = 234 + 20b$
$$b = \frac{491 - 234}{20} = 12.85$$
so C

9 In the equation $Y = a + bx$, a is equal to the intercept
so A

10 For a perfect positive correlation we want the value of R to be equal to 1.
so B

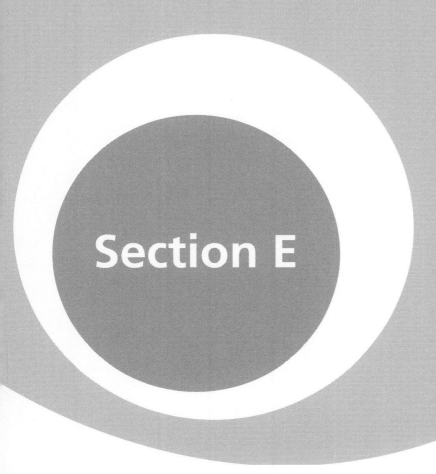

Section E

Forecasting

14

Time Series

Time Series

14

? Concepts, definitions and short-form questions

1 An inflation index and a sales index of a company's sales for the last year are as follows:

Quarter	1	2	3	4
Sales index	109	120	132	145
Inflation index	100	110	121	133

Calculate the real value of sales for quarter 4.

2 Give an example of one of the following

- (i) long-term trend
- (ii) cyclical variation
- (iii) seasonal variation
- (iv) random variation

3 In an additive time series model $A = T + C + S + R$, the initials stand for

- (i) A
- (ii) T
- (iii) C
- (iv) S
- (v) R

? Questions 4–7 are based on the following information

The takings (in '000s) at Mr Li's Takeaway for the past 16 quarters are as follows:

Quarter	1	2	3	4
2000	13	22	58	23
2001	16	28	61	25
2002	17	29	61	26
2003	18	30	65	29

4 Calculate the four quarterly moving average.

5 Calculate the trend.

125

6   Calculate the quarterly variation.

7   If Mr Li thinks his takings for the four quarters in 2004 will be £19,000, £32,000, £65,000 and £30,000, has the upward trend continued?

8   A product has a constant trend in its sales and is subject to the following quarterly seasonal variations.

Quarter	Q_1	Q_2	Q_3	Q_4
Seasonality	+50%	+50%	−50%	−50%

Assuming a multiplicative model for the time series, what should sales be for quarter 3, if sales in last quarter, Q^2, were 240?

9   Based on the last 18 periods, the underlying sales trend is $y = 345 - 1.5x$. If the seasonal factor for period 19 is −23.5, if we assume an additive forecasting model, what is the forecast for period 19?

10 Over the past 15 months, sales have had an underlying linear trend of $y = 7.5 + 3.8x$ where y is the number of items sold and x is the month of sale. Month 16 is expected to be 1.12 times the trend value.
    What is the sales forecast for month 19?

✓ Concepts, definitions and short-form solutions

1   Quarter 4 $= \dfrac{145}{133} \times 100 = 109$ same as Quarter 1

2   (i)   change in population
    (ii)   down turn in economic activity
    (iii) rise in goods sold before Christmas
    (iv)   events in New York September 11th 2001

3   A = actual value for the period
    T = trend component
    C = cyclical component
    S = seasonal component
    R = residual component

4   1st quarter   =   13
                       22
                       58
                       23
                       ——
                       116 ÷ 4 = 29
    2nd quarter   =   22
                       58
                       23
                       16
                       ——
                       119 ÷ 4 = 30
    So 29, 30, 31, 34, 33, 33, 33, 33, 33, 34, 34, 35, 36

5   Trend equals central value of four quarterly moving average
    So 1st trend   = 29 + 30
         2nd trend   = 30 + 31
    So rounded up 30, 31, 32, 33, 33, 33, 33, 33, 34, 34, 35, 36

6   Quarter 1   −16
    Quarter 2   −5
    Quarter 3   29
    Quarter 4   −8

7   19 − (−16)   35
    32 − (−5)   37
    65 − 29   36
    30 − (−8)   38
    Yes, upward trend has continued

8   Forecast = T × S
    Sales last quarter 240 Q^2
    Seasonally for Q^2 = +50   ∴ S = 150

    $\text{Trend} = \dfrac{240}{150} \times 100 = 160$

    Seasonality = −50% S = 50

    $\text{Forecast} = \dfrac{160 \times 50}{100} = 80$

9   $y = 345 − 1.5x$
    $x = 19$ so $y = 345 − 28.5 = 316.5$
    Seasonally adjusted 316.5 − 23.5 = 293

10 $y = 7.5 + 3.8x$
    Seasonal variation = 1.12 × trend
    For month 19 y = (7.5 + 3.8 × 16) 1.12
                        = (7.5 + 60.8) 1.12
                        = 68.3 × 1.12
              y = 76.5

❓ Multiple choice questions

Questions 1–5 are based on the following information

The figures below relate to the number of daily visitors to an hotel aggregated by quarter.

	Quarter 1	Quarter 2	Quarter 3	Quarter 4
2000	–	–	–	88
2001	90	120	200	28
2002	22	60	164	16
2003	10	80	192	–

1   The first figure to go in the 4th quarter total is

    A   498
    B   438
    C   428
    D   418

2   The first figure to go in the 8th quarter total is

    A   900
    B   918
    C   936
    D   950

3   The average seasonal variation for the first quarter in 2002 was

    A   −3
    B   −1
    C   1
    D   3

4   What is the expected number of daily visitors for the 4th quarter of 2003 if trend figures is 120?

    A   30
    B   40
    C   45
    D   50

5   Based on the last 15 periods, the underlying sales trend is $y = 345.12 - 1.35x$.
If the 16th period has a seasonal factor of -23.62, assuming an additive forecasting model, then the forecast for the period is

    A   275
    B   300
    C   325
    D   350

6   Over an 18 month period, sales have been found to have an underlying linear trend of $y = 7.112 + 3.949x$ where y is the number of items sold and x represents the month. Monthly deviations from trend have been calculated and month 19 is expected to be 1.12 times the trend value. The forecast number of items to be sold in month 19 is

    A   88
    B   90
    C   92
    D   94

7   The influence of booms and slumps in an industry is a measure of

    A   long-term trends
    B   cyclical variations
    C   seasonal variations
    D   random variations

8   An inflation index and index numbers of a company's sales (£) for the last year are given below.

Quarter	1	2	3	4
Sales (£) index	109	120	132	145
Inflation index	100	110	121	133

'Real' sales that is, adjusted for inflation are

A   approximately constant and keeping up with inflation
B   growing steadily and not keeping up with inflation
C   growing steadily and keeping ahead of inflation
D   falling steadily and not keeping up with inflation

9   A product has a constant (flat) trend in its sales, and is subject to quarterly seasonal variations as follows:

Quarter	Q_1	Q_2	Q_3	Q_4
Seasonality	+50%	+50%	−50%	−50%

Sales last quarter, Q_2, were 240 units.

Assuming a multiplicative model for the time series, predicted unit sales for the next quarter, Q_3, will be closest to

A   60
B   80
C   120
D   160

✓ Multiple choice solutions

1   88
   90
 120
 <u>200</u>
 498
so A

2   498 +   90
       120
       200
        <u>28</u>
     438 = 936
so C

3   8th quarter total   = 936
8th quarter average = 117
actual 2nd quarter   = 120
variation   =   3
so D

4

	Average	Seasonal variations		
	Q_1	Q_2	Q_3	Q_4
2001		+3	+99	−57
2002	−51	−7	+100	−49
2003	−61			
Total	−112	−4	+199	−106
Mean	−56	−2	+99.5	−52
Mean =	−11.5			
Adjusted mean	−53	+1	+102	−50

Best estimate = trend − seasonal variation
$$= 120 - 70 = 50$$

so D

5   $x = 16$
$$= 345.12 - 1.35(16) \quad = 323.52$$
    seasonally adjusted $= -23.62$ so 300
so B

6   $y = 7.112 + 3.949x$
seasonal variation = $1.12 \times$ trend
for month 19
$y = 7.112 + (3.949 \times 19) \, 1.12$
$y = 92$
so C

7   The influence of booms and slumps in an industry is a measure of cyclical variations
so B

8   Quarter real sales

1   $\dfrac{109}{100} \times 100 = 109.0$

2   $\dfrac{120}{110} \times 100 = 109.1$

3   $\dfrac{132}{121} \times 100 = 109.1$

4   $\dfrac{145}{133} \times 100 = 109.0$

The real series is approximately constant and keeping up with inflation.
so A

9   Multiplicative model forecast $= T \times S$
     Sales last quarter 240 (Q_2)
     Seasonality for $Q_2 = +50\%$ $S = 150$

     Trend $= \dfrac{240}{150} \times 100 = 160$ for Q_3

     Seasonality $= -50\%$ $S = 50$

     Forecast $= 160 \times \dfrac{50}{100} = 80$

     so B

Section F

Financial Mathematics

Financial Mathematics

Financial Mathematics

15

? Concepts, definitions and short-form questions

1   A boy is given £100 from his grandmother on the 1st January each year. On 31st December simple interest is credited at 10% which he withdraws to spend. How much will be in the account on 31st December after five years?

2   If the boy kept the interest and credited it to his account each year, how much would be in the account on 31st December after five years if £100 was invested in year 1 but no more payments received after that?

3   A new machine costs £5,000 and is depreciated by 8% per annum. What is the book value of the machine after five years?

4   A new machine costs £8,000 and lasts 10 years and has a scrap value of £100. What is the annual rate of compound depreciation?

5   Dougie is saving to pay for his daughter's wedding in five years' time. He puts £400 per year in the bank which will earn interest at 9%. The wedding is expected to cost £3,000. Will he have saved up enough by then?

6   How much needs to be invested now at 6% per annum to provide an annuity of £5,000 per annum for ten years commencing in five years' time?

7   Calculate the annual repayment on a bank loan of £50,000 over eight years at 9% per annum.

8   How much needs to be invested now at 5% to yield an annual income of £10,000 in perpetuity?

9   An initial investment of £2,000 yields yearly cash flows of £500, £500, £600, £600 and £440 at the end of each year. At the end of year five, there is no scrap value. If capital is available at 12%, using discounted cash flow and internal rate of return assess whether the project should be accepted.

10   If a credit card company has an annual percentage rate (APR) of 30% how much interest are they charging a customer each month?

137

✓ Concepts, definitions and short-form solutions

1   *Year*   *Investment £*

    1   100
    2   200
    3   300
    4   400
    5   500
    So £500

2   *Year*   *Principal £*   *Interest £*   *Total £*

    1   100   10   110
    2   110   11   121
    3   121   12.10   133.10
    4   133.10   13.31   146.41
    5   146.41   14.64   161.05

3   $x = £5,000$

    $r = 8\% = \dfrac{8}{100} = 0.08 \quad n = 5$

    $D = x(1-r)^n = £5,000 \times (1-0.08)^5 = £5,000 \times 0.6591$
    $= £3,295$

4   $D = £100 \qquad x = £8,000 \qquad n = 10$
    so $100 = 8,000 (1 - r)^{10}$

    $(1 - r)^{10} = \dfrac{100}{8,000} = 0.0125$

    $(1 - r) = \sqrt[10]{0.0125}$
    $= 0.6452$
    $r = 1 - 0.6452 = 0.3548 = 35.48\%$

5   Assume first instalment is paid immediately

    $S_n = \dfrac{A(R^n - 1)}{R - 1}$ where A = annual savings $R = 1.09$ $n = 6$
    S_n is the amount saved after 6 years

    $= \dfrac{£400 \times (1.09^6 - 1)}{1.09}$

    $= £3,009$

6   See annuity table. Check values of 6% at year 14 and year 4
    PV = £5,000 (year 14 − year 4)
    $= £5,000 (9.295 - 3.465)$
    $= £29,150$

7   Again go straight to cumulative present value and look up the value for 9% at eight years = 5.535

    so $\dfrac{£50,000}{5.535} = £9,033.42$ per annum

8   Present value of perpetuity is $£10,000 \times \dfrac{1}{0.05} = £200,000.$

9   Net present value

Year	Cash flow £	DCF-12%	Present value
0	(2,000)	1	(2,000)
1	500	0.893	447
2	500	0.797	399
3	600	0.712	427
4	600	0.636	382
5	440	0.567	249

Net present value − £96
Internal rate of return 8%

Year	Cash flow £	DCF-8%	Present value
0	(2,000)	1	(2,000)
1	500	0.926	463
2	500	0.857	429
3	600	0.794	476
4	600	0.735	441
5	440	0.681	300

Net present value = £109
IRR is between 12% and 8%

So IRR $= A + \left(\dfrac{NA}{NA - NB}\right) \times B - A$

$= 8\% + \left(\dfrac{109}{109 - (-96)}\right) \times (12\% - 8\%)$

$= 8\% + \left(\dfrac{109}{2.5}\right) \times 4\%$

$= 10.13\%$

Reject NPV because at 12% it is negative.
Reject IRR because it is below 12%.

10   $(1 + r)^{12} = 1.30$
There are 12 months in a year
So $1+r = \sqrt[12]{1.3} = 2.21$
   So $r = 2.21\%$

? Multiple choice questions

1   A credit card company is charging an annual percentage rate of 25.3%. This is equivalent
to a monthly rate of

A   1.8
B   1.9
C   2.0
D   2.2

2 Johnny receives £1,000 per annum starting today and receives five such payments. If the rate of interest is 8% what is the net present value of this income stream?

    A   £4,000
    B   £4,100
    C   £4,282
    D   £4,312

3 A new machine costs £5,000 and is depreciated by 8% per annum. The book value of the machine in five years time will be

    A   £5,000
    B   £4,219
    C   £3,295
    D   £2,970

4 Which is worth most, at present values, assuming an annual rate of interest of 12%?

    A   £1,200 one year from now
    B   £1,400 two years from now
    C   £1,600 three years from now
    D   £1,800 four years from now

5 A landlord receives a rent of £1,000 to be received over ten successive years. The first payment is due now. If interest rates are 8% then the present value of this income is equal to

    A   £6,250
    B   £6,973
    C   £7,247
    D   £7,915

6 If interest rates are 8%, which is worth most at present values?

    A   £1,200 one year from now
    B   £1,400 two years from now
    C   £1,600 three years from now
    D   £1,800 four years from now

7 How much would need to be invested today at 6% per annum to provide an annuity of £5,000 per annum for ten years commencing in five years' time?

    A   £5,000
    B   £19,000
    C   £29,150
    D   £39,420

8 What is the annual repayment on a bank loan of £50,000 over eight years at 9%?

    A   £8,975
    B   £9,033
    C   £9,214
    D   £9,416

9 How much needs to be invested now at 5% to yield an annual income of £4,000 in perpetuity?

   A   £80,000
   B   £90,000
   C   £100,000
   D   £120,000

✓ Multiple choice solutions

1 $(1 + r)^{12} = 1.25$
There are 12 months in a year.
so $1 + r = \sqrt[12]{1.25} = 1.9$
so B

2 £1,000 (1 + cumulative factor for year 4 at 8%)
= £1,000 (1 + 3.312)
= £4,312
so D

3 $x = £5,000$

  $r = 8\% = \dfrac{8}{100} = 0.08$

  $D = x (1 - r)^n$
     $= £5,000 \times (1 - 0.08)^5$
     $= £5,000 \times 0.6591$
     $= £3,295$
so C

4 £1,200/1.12   = £1,071
£1,400/(1.12)² = £1,116
£1,600/(1.12)³ = £1,139
£1,800/(1.12)⁴ = £1,144
so D

5 NPV = £1,000 (1 + 6.247)
       = £1,000 × 7.247
       = £7,247
so C

6 A = £1,200/1.08   = £1,111.20
  B = £1,400/(1.08)² = £1,199.80
  C = £1,600/(1.08)³ = £1,273.40
  D = £1,800/(1.08)⁴ = £1,323.00
so D

7 Check cumulative present value table
6% year 14   9.295
6% year 4   3.465   subtract
                 5.830
£5,000 × 5.830 = £29,150
so C

8   Let x = annual repayment
Present value of 8 repayments of x at 9% = £50,000
From tables 5.535 × x = £50,000

$$x = \frac{£50,000}{5.535} = £9,033$$

so B

9   A real life example of this is a pension. In other words you are living off the interest and the capital remains.

$$£4,000 \times \frac{1}{0.05} = £80,000$$

so A

Section G

Spreadsheets

Spreadsheets

Spreadsheets

16

Question 1

	A	B	C	D	E
1	Values for x	$y = x^2 + 5x + 10$			
2	−25	510			
3	−20	310			
4	−15	160			
5	−10	60			
6	−5	10			
7	0	10			
8	5	60			
9	10	160			
10	15	310			
11	20	510			

The above data is to be plotted onto a labelled graph in Excel.

What shape will the resulting graph be?

(A)   A curve with a maximum point
(B)   A straight line with a change of gradient, where $x = 0$
(C)   A curve with a minimum point
(D)   Curved but the number of minimum or maximum points cannot be predicted without further calculations

(2 marks)

Question 2

The following data is to be used to create a pie chart in Excel.

	A	B	C	D	E
1			£		
2		18–25	59.3		
3		26–35	61.6		
4		36–45	10.3		
5		46–55	15.8		
6		56 and over	9.9		
7		Total	156.9		
8					
9					
10					
11					

What range should be selected?

(A) B2:C7
(B) A2:C6
(C) B2:C6
(D) The data cannot be used to create a pie chart without alteration

(2 marks)

Question 3

Which of the following are principles of good spreadsheet design?

(i) Build in cross-checks to validate data/calculations
(ii) Use absolute values in formulae
(iii) Keep graphs on separate chart sheets where possible
(iv) Use colour coded fonts on larger plans

   (A) (i) and (iii)
   (B) (i), (ii) and (iii)
   (C) (i), (ii), (iii) and (iv)
   (D) (i), (iii) and (iv)

(2 marks)

Question 4

If the formula =NOW() is entered into an Excel spreadsheet:

(A) Only the current date will be displayed in the cell
(B) Only the current time will be displayed in the cell
(C) Both the current time and date will be displayed in the cell
(D) The display in the cell will depend on whether DATE, TIME or DATETIME is typed between the brackets

(2 marks)

Question 5

	A	B	C	D
1	BORROWING RATES AND LOANS			
2				
3	Loan rate (%)	Amount outstanding		Forecast
4	8.00	12050		
5	8.25	12600		
6	8.50	12835		
7	8.50	12200		
8	8.75	13060		
9	9.00	13500		
10	9.25	13100		
11	9.25	13300		
12	9.25	13500		
13	9.50	14100		

The formula =FORECAST(A4,$B$4:$B$13,$A$4:$A$13) is to be entered into cell D4.

(A)   It can now be copied into cells D5 through D13, and the resulting data used to plot the line of least squares (i.e. a regression line)

(B)   It can now be copied into cells D5 through D13, and the resulting data used to calculate a frequency distribution

(C)   The formula should have the fixed cell references removed so it can then be copied into cells D5 through D13, and the resulting data used to plot the line of least squares (i.e. a regression line)

(D)   The formula should have the fixed cell references removed so it can then be copied into cells D5 through D13, and the resulting data used to calculate a frequency distribution

(2 marks)

Question 6

	A	B	C	D
1	Product line	Sales £'000		
2	Soups	1200		
3	Tinned vegetables	600		
4	Sauces	450		
5	Salad dressings	900		
6	Tinned stews	550		
7	Condiments	200		
8	Tinned pasta	1700		
9	Total	5600		
10				
11				
12				

The above data is to be analysed. To perform the analysis the following actions will be carried out:

1. Sort the data by descending size.
2. Calculate the percentage of the total that each item represents.
3. Find the cumulative percentage sales each item contributes.

This analysis is known as

(A) Regression analysis
(B) Pareto analysis
(C) Frequency distribution analysis
(D) Standard deviation and probability analysis

(2 marks)

Question 7

	A	B	C	D
1		Cash flows		
2				
3	Initial investment	350000		
4	Year 1	60000		
5	Year 2	95000		
6	Year 3	120000		
7	Year 4	180000		
8	Year 5	200000		
9				
10	Interest rate	0.2		
11				
12				

Which of the following formula will correctly calculate the NPV of the above investment?

(A) =NPV(B10,B4:B8)−B3
(B) =NPV(B10,B4:B8)+B3
(C) =NPV(B10,B3:B8)
(D) =NPV(B10,SUM(−B3,B4:B8))

(2 marks)

Question 8

	A	B	C	D	E
1					
2	Amount invested	368000			
3	Cash flow year 1	48000			
4	Cash flow year 2	27000			
5	Cash flow year 3	32000			
6	Cash flow year 4	19000			
7					
8	Fixed cost of capital	12%			
9					
10					

The formula below (without the missing data) was entered into cell B10 and the answer was 0.09.

Identify the contents of the blanks in the formula =ROUND(• (B3:B6)/B2, •)

(A) • IRR   • 1
(B) • AVERAGE   • 2
(C) • NPV   • 1
(D) • ROI   • 2

(2 marks)

✓ Multiple choice answers

Answer 1

The answer is (C)

Working

The values of y first fall and then rise again symmetrically over the range of values given for x. This will result in a curve with a minimum point.

Answer 2

The answer is (C)

Working

The data in row 7 must not be included, otherwise the total will be treated as another result and will be allocated its own piece of pie. The range should only include those columns containing the actual data to be used.

Answer 3

The answer is (D)

Working

The use of absolute values is to be kept to a minimum as they do not change in line with changes in the assumptions which makes 'what–if?'analysis harder to perform.

Answer 4

The answer is (C)

Working

The formula =NOW() is typed into the required cell and the time and date as set on the computer will be inserted into the spreadsheet.

Answer 5

The answer is (A)

Working

=FORECAST is the function used to plot a regression line. The fixed cell references are necessary to ensure that each observation is compared with the whole range.

Answer 6

The answer is (B)

Working

Pareto analysis is based on the 80:20 rule, which can be expanded into a business setting, as the knowledge that a small number of items may take up a disproportionate amount of time. The above analysis of sales would identify the items that represent about 80% of revenue – the implication being that most business attention should focus on them.

Answer 7

The answer is (A)

Working

The initial investment must be expressed separately as it does not need to be discounted. It would otherwise be treated as the first year's cash flow. It must be deducted here because it has been expressed as a positive figure in the data table.

Answer 8

The answer is (B)

Working

Average is the Excel term used to calculate the ROI. Neither NPV nor IRR would require the figures to be divided by cell contents as in the formula here. The answer is rounded to two decimal places so the second blank must be 2.

❓ Concepts, definitions and short-form questions

Question 1

What formula should be entered into the appropriate cell in the following worksheet to calculate the median number of televisions sold to one decimal place? How would it change if the mode was required?

	A	B	C	D	E
1	Average weekly televisions sold				
2	36	32	33	33	
3	33	38	35	37	
4	35	39	36	36	
5	32	37	37	32	
6	38	34	38	34	
7	35	35	34	37	
8					
9					
10					

Question 2

Complete the formula to be entered into cell C4 to calculate the compound interest rate if it is to be copied into cells C5 to C8?

	A	B	C	D	E
1	Investment amount	450000			
2	Interest rate	9%			
3					
4	Year number	1			
5		2			
6		3			
7		4			
8		5			
9					
10					

Question 3

	A	B	C	D	E
1	Amount invested	−250000			
2	Cash flow year 1	90000			
3	Cash flow year 2	35000			
4	Cash flow year 3	52000			
5	Cash flow year 4	19000			
6					
7	Fixed cost of capital	5%			
8					
9					
10					

(i) What is the Excel function and formulae required to calculate the NPV on the above investment?

(ii) Rewrite the formula to calculate the IRR (assuming a figure of 10% will be used for your first guess). You are not required to fix any cell references.

Question 4

The following calculations needs to be performed in an Excel spreadsheet.

(i) $38 \div 3 \times 42.3^2$ to three decimal places

(ii) $\sqrt{220} \times 4^2$ to the nearest whole number

What should be entered in the appropriate cells in the worksheet?

Question 5

What linear regression formula should be entered into cell C2 to forecast the growth of plants for a given level of rainfall if it is to be copied into cells C3 to C7?

	A	B	C	D	E
1	Rainfall (mm)	Plant growth (cm)			
2	30	110			
3	34	115			
4	38	115			
5	30	110			
6	42	120			
7	50	120			
8					

Question 6

List *five* principles of good spreadsheet design

Question 7

Define the following terms:

  (i)   Cells
 (ii)   Workbooks
(iii)   Worksheets
(iv)   Macros

Question 8

What is the difference between formatting a cell to two decimal places and using the =ROUND function with '2' after the required function?

Question 9

What is a template of a business plan? What advantages would it provide?

Question 10

List the Business Mathematics functions that you remember that can be performed in Excel?

Question 11

A chain of regional garden centres has been monitoring the relationship between sales figures and advertising spend. The following information has been established:

	A	B	C	D	
1	Region	Advertising spend £(000s)	Sales revenue £(000s)		
2	North West	12.5	31.25		
3	North East	14.3	30.03		
4	Midlands	16.7	37.91		
5	South East	14.4	33.12		
6	South West	11.7	24.57		
7	London	13.5	25.52		

Run through the key steps you would need to follow, in order to create a line of least squares in Excel.

Question 12

A local scout group has traditionally put together its budgets for various sections (beavers, cubs and scouts) on paper and then used them to draw up a group budget for approval by the Executive Committee. Recently, a fund-raising event raised enough money for a group laptop and it has been agreed that the budgets will now be drawn up using Excel. The section leaders are not sure what Excel can do and are concerned that they will now have significant extra work to do every year.

You are the treasurer of the scout group, so it has fallen to you to explain the benefits to the group that this method will bring and to suggest how the section leaders might best go about preparing their budgets so that they can minimise the work needed.

Write brief notes for the next group meeting which explain:

(a) The benefits of using Excel
(b) How the budgets can be drawn up to reduce the workload

You can assume that the leaders understand basic Excel terminology

Question 13

Your firm is planning an investment which will cost £50,000 immediately. It should return cash flows over the next 5 years of £12,000, £15,000, £14,000, £22,000 and £18,000 respectively.

(a) Find the NPV at a cost of capital of 10% and advise the firm whether to accept the project on this basis
(b) Find the IRR and advise the firm whether to accept the project on this basis
(c) Enter the data into the blank spreadsheet below and show the formula needed to calculate the NPV and IRR using Excel.

	A	B
1		
2		
3		
4		
5		
6		
7		
8		
9		
10		
11	NPV =	
12	IRR =	

Answer 1

The answer is

=ROUND(MEDIAN(A2:D7),1)

Working

The ROUND function that encircles the basic MEDIAN function is there to set the number of decimal places – here to just one place. Remember that formatting the cell will only change the displayed number of decimal places not the actual value held.

If the mode were required rather than the median, the formula would become

=ROUND(MODE(A2:D7),1)

Answer 2

The answer is

=$B$1*(1+$B$2)^B4

Working

The references to the cells containing the amount invested and the interest rate must be fixed to prevent them being altered as the formula is copied.

Answer 3

The NPV would be calculated as

= NPV(B7,B2:B5)+B1

Working

The investment figure has been entered into the spreadsheet as a negative figure here and must therefore be added to the discounted cash flows.

The IRR would be

=IRR(B1:B5)

Working

NB If the calculation did not work, resulting in the answer #NUM!, it would be necessary to add an alternative guess to the 10% used as a default such as 20%, that is =IRR(B1:B5,0.2)

Answer 4

(i)   =ROUND(38/3*42.3^2,3)
(ii) =ROUND(SQRT(220)*4^2,0)
NB Alternatively you can also set 220 to the power of a half: =ROUND(220^(1/2)*4^2,0)

Answer 5

The answer is

=FORECAST(A2,$B$2:$B$7,$A$2:$A$7)

Working

Note that the first cell is not fixed as that will need to alter to reflect the actual level of rainfall in each row. However the cells marking the range of findings against which it is plotted are fixed.

Answer 6

(i) Build in cross-checks to validate data/calculations
(ii) Keep the use absolute values in formulae to a minimum
(iii) Keep graphs on separate chart sheets where possible
(iv) Use colour coded fonts on larger plans
(v) Ensure the worksheets are labelled and dated.

Answer 7

(i) Worksheets are described using column letters and row numbers. Each row/column co-ordinate is referred to as a *cell* and each cell has a unique address. For example, the cell where column C and row 8 intersect is referred to as cell C8. Cell references are used in the creation of formulae.
(ii) An Excel file is called a *workbook*. A workbook can consist of a single *worksheet* or a combination of multiple worksheets, charts, databases and so on.
(iii) A *worksheet* is a grid of rows and columns, forming a series of cells. Most of the work done in Excel will be done on worksheets.
(iv) *Macros* are the record of a series of keystrokes or mouse clicks.

Answer 8

Formatting a cell changes the display so that only 2 decimal places are viewed. It is important to remember that cells that are formatted still hold the data as before and if calculations are performed on them will use the pure number not the one on display. The =ROUND function must be used to actually round the data held in the cell. Calculations performed on the data will then use the rounded figure.

Answer 9

A template is a plan that contains the logic required for the plan to work but with all the data removed. When new data is entered then the plan is created.

Advantages include:

- Business plans take time to design and create. The template stores this effort for future use.
- Using a template ensures that plans made at different times or for different departments are directly comparable.
- Preparing the template will help identify any inappropriate use of absolute values which can be rectified for future use.
- New plans can be drawn up far more quickly.

Answer 10

Excel can perform over 350 functions. Some of those that have been covered in the syllabus include:

- Plotting graphs of equations
- Drawing graphs (histograms, ogives, pie charts) to present data
- Calculation of statistical functions such as standard deviation and variance
- Calculation of NPV and IRR
- Drawing scatter diagrams
- Plotting the line of least squares
- 'What–if?' analysis.

Answer 11

First a scatter diagram needs to be created using the data gathered.

This is done by selecting the range containing the data (here B2:C7), and using the chart icon to select an *XY* scatter chart

Next, a least squares column is needed.

For this, we need to identify the independent variable – here the data in column B, and then set up the forecast function. The range is fixed using $ signs, and linked to each independent variable in turn. Note that the dependent variables are specified before the dependent ones when the range is given:

	A	B	C	D
1	Region	Advertising spend £(000s)	Sales revenue £(000s)	Least squared line
2	North West	12.5	31.25	=FORECAST(B2,$C$2:$C$7,$B$2:$B$7)
3	North East	14.3	30.03	=FORECAST(B3,$C$2:$C$7,$B$2:$B$7)
4	Midlands	16.7	37.91	=FORECAST(B4,$C$2:$C$7,$B$2:$B$7)
5	South East	14.4	33.12	=FORECAST(B5,$C$2:$C$7,$B$2:$B$7)
6	South West	11.7	24.57	=FORECAST(B6,$C$2:$C$7,$B$2:$B$7)
7	London	13.5	25.52	=FORECAST(B7,$C$2:$C$7,$B$2:$B$7)

The least squares column (D2:D7) can now be copied onto the chart.

Finally, by selecting one of the data symbols and setting Line to Automatic, the line is revealed.

Answer 12

(a) The benefits to the Scout Group of using Excel:

- Avoids the need for manual calculations – quicker and more accurate
- By using calculation cross-checks, any missing data can be quickly identified
- Once individual budgets have been drawn up (probably on separate worksheets within a workbook), they can be simply combined into an annual group budget.
- 'What–if' analysis can be performed. For example, the impact of additional children joining, or a lower than expected amount raised from a fund-raising event, can be simply analysed.
- If leaders need to explain any assumptions they have made, they can be simply included by means of a 'Comment' inserted into a cell.
- The budgets drawn up this year will provide a working template to reduce work significantly in future years.

(b) How the budgets can be drawn up to reduce the workload:

- It would be worth agreeing a common format for each section, to simplify the process of drawing together the information into a group budget.
- To avoid confusion, the rows and columns should be clearly labelled and colour coded as necessary
- All absolute values should be kept in a separate data table away from the main part of the budget. The budget should then be created using formula, which use the data in the table as needed. This will ensure that the impact of any changes to the estimates when put through into the data table will immediately flow through into the budget.
- Once the budget for the year has been created, a copy should be made. The data in the table is removed and the cells containing the formula protected. This Template can then be used to draw up future year's budgets more quickly.
- To avoid minor mathematical variations due to rounding, the formula should be set to round to two decimal places. Note that it is not enough to format the cells, since this changes the display but not the underlying value held.

Answer 13

Time	Cash flow	DF @ 10%	PV @ 10%	DF @ 20%	PV @ 20%
T_0	(50,000)	1	(50,000)	1	(50,000)
T_1	12,000	0.909	10,908	0.833	9,996
T_2	15,000	0.826	12,390	0.694	10,410
T_3	14,000	0.751	10,514	0.597	8,358
T_4	22,000	0.683	15,026	0.482	10,604
T_5	18,000	0.621	11,178	0.402	7,236
	Total NPV		10,016		(3,396)

The NPV at 10% is £10,016 and the investment should be accepted.

$$IRR = R_1 + \left[(R_2 - R_1) \times \frac{NPV_1}{NPV - NPV_2} \right]$$

$$IRR = 10 + \left[(20 - 10) \times \frac{10,016}{10,016 - (3,396)} \right]$$

$$IRR = 10 + \left[10 \times \frac{10,016}{13,412} \right]$$

$$IRR = 10 + [10 \times 0.7467]$$

$$IRR = 10 + 7.47 = 17.5\%$$

The IRR is above the cost of capital of 10% which also leads to the conclusion that the project should be accepted.

Obviously the cash flows can be entered into any column of cells. The purpose here is to clarify the range that is being included in the NPV and IRR formulae.

	A	B
1		
2	Time	Cash flows
3	T_0	−50000
4	T_1	12000
5	T_2	15000
6	T_3	14000
7	T_4	22000
8	T_5	18000
9		
10	Cost of capital	10%
11	NPV =	= NPV(B10,B4:B8) + B3
12	IRR =	=IRR(B3:B8)

Section H

Mock Assessment

Mock Assessment

Mock Assessment **17**

Instructions to students

You have 2 hours in which to complete this assessment.

You may attempt all questions. Mathematical tables and formulae are available.

Do not turn the page until you are ready to attempt the assessment under timed conditions.

? Question 1

Use the following data about the production of faulty or acceptable items in three departments to answer the probability questions. All items referred to in the questions are randomly selected from this sample of 250. Give all answers correct to four d.p.

| | *Department* | | | |
	P	*Q*	*R*	*Total*
Faulty	7	10	15	32
Acceptable	46	78	94	218
Total	53	88	109	250

(A) What is the probability that an item is faulty?
    Answer ⬚

(B) What is the probability that an item from department P is faulty?
    Answer ⬚

(C) What is the probability that an item found to be faulty comes from department P?
    Answer ⬚

(6 marks)

? Question 2

In an additive model, the seasonal variations given by averaging $Y - T$ values are 25, 18, -5 and -30. They have to be adjusted so that their total is 0. What is the value after adjustment of the average currently valued at -30?

Answer ⬚   **(2 marks)**

? Question 3

Which of the following examples would constitute a multiple bar chart?

(A) Three adjacent bars then a gap then another three bars.
(B) Six separate bars.
(C) Two bars with a gap between them, each divided into three sections.
(D) Any bar chart which displays more than one variable.

Answer ⬚   **(2 marks)**

? Question 4

If $\Sigma x = 500$, $\Sigma y = 200$, $\Sigma x^2 = 35,000$, $\Sigma y^2 = 9,000$, $\Sigma xy = 12,000$ and $n = 10$, calculate the product moment correlation coefficient to three d.p.

Answer ⬚   **(2 marks)**

❓ Question 5

Which of the following statements about standard deviation is incorrect?

(A) It measures variability.
(B) It uses all the data.
(C) It is not distorted by skewed data.
(D) Its formula lends itself to mathematical manipulation.

Answer ☐   **(2 marks)**

❓ Question 6

An investment rises in value from £12,000 to £250,000 over 15 years. Calculate the percentage increase per year, to one d.p.

Answer ☐   **(2 marks)**

❓ Question 7

Events P and Q are said to be independent. What does this mean?

(A) If P occurs, Q cannot occur
(B) If P occurs the probability of Q occurring is unchanged
(C) If P occurs the probability of Q occurring is 0
(D) If P occurs the probability of Q occurring is 1.

Answer ☐   **(2 marks)**

❓ Question 8

A wages distribution is as follows

Weekly wages (£)	Frequency	cf
100 and less than 200	5	..
200 and less than 300	20	..
300 and less than 400	55	..
400 and less than 500	18	..
500 or more	2	..

(A) Write the cumulative (less than) frequencies in the cf column.
(B) What is the cumulative frequency of the upper quartile?
Answer ☐   **(4 marks)**

❓ Question 9

Sales figures are given as 547,000 but after seasonal adjustment using a multiplicative model they are only 495,000. Calculate the seasonal component for the particular season, to 3 d.p.

Answer ☐   **(2 marks)**

? Question 10

A sample is taken by randomly selecting from the staff in each department, with sample numbers in proportion to the numbers employed in the various departments. What is such a sample called?

(A) Systematic
(B) Simple random
(C) Stratified random
(D) Quota.

Answer ☐   **(2 marks)**

? Question 11

If a sum of £15,000 is invested at 4.6 per cent per annum, find its value after 5 years, to the nearest £.

Answer ☐   **(2 marks)**

? Question 12

(A) Express the following average weekly wages as index numbers with base 1998, to 1 d.p.

Year	97	98	99	2000	2001	2002
RPI	166	172	178	184	190	197
Wages	414	426	440	450	468	480
Index	...	...	...	...	...	...

(B) If the index for 2003 were to be 116 and the RPI 204, express the index for 2003 at constant 1998 prices.

(C) If the average wages index for 2003 at constant 1998 prices were to be 96, which of the following comments would be correct?

(A) Average wages in 2003 could buy 4 per cent less than in 1998
(B) Average wages in 2003 could buy 4 per cent more than in 1998
(C) Average wages in 2003 were 4 per cent more than in 1998
(D) Average prices in 2003 were 4 per cent less than in 1998

Answer ☐   **(6 marks)**

? Question 13

The expression $(x^3)^2/x^4$ equals

(A) $1/x$
(B) 1
(C) x
(D) x^2

Answer ☐   **(2 marks)**

⁇ **Question 14**

If Q is given as 34 with a possible error of $\pm 2\%$ and R is given as 6.5 with a possible error of $\pm 4\%$, find the largest possible true value of Q/R to 3 d.p.

Answer ☐   **(2 marks)**

⁇ **Question 15**

The pass rate for a particular exam is 48 per cent. In a randomly selected group of three students, find the probabilities (to 4 d.p.) that

(A) No one passes
Answer ☐

(B) All three pass
Answer ☐   **(4 marks)**

⁇ **Question 16**

A company has to choose between borrowing £100,000 at 3 per cent a quarter in order to modernise now or saving at 2 per cent a quarter in order to modernise in 4 years time, at an estimated cost of £117,000. Throughout this question, use tables whenever possible.

(A) Find the cumulative discount factor appropriate to quarter end payments of £1 per quarter at 3 per cent per quarter over 5 years.
Answer ☐

(B) Calculate the amount £X which must be paid per quarter if the company borrows £100,000 now repayable at the end of each quarter over 4 years. Give your answer correct to the nearest £.
Answer ☐

(C) Calculate the amount £Y which must be saved at the end of each quarter if the company wishes to cover the cost of modernisation in 4 years time. Give your answer to the nearest £.
Answer ☐   **(6 marks)**

⁇ **Question 17**

Eight samples of wine have been listed in order of taste (with the best taste being ranked number one) and their prices are also listed.

Sample taste	1	2	3	4	5	6	7	8
Price (£)	6.99	4.95	5.99	5.99	4.49	3.99	2.99	2.99
Rank of price	..	..	..	..	..	..	..	..

(A) Rank the prices of the wines with the lowest price being ranked number one.
(B) If the differences in corresponding ranks are denoted by 'd' and if $\Sigma d^2 = 150$, calculate Spearman's rank correlation coefficient to 3 d.p.
Answer ☐

(C) If the rank correlation coefficient was -0.9, which of the following statements would be correct?

(D) There is a strong link between price and taste.

(E) There is a strong linear relationship between price and taste.

(F) Taste rank increases as price gets higher.

(G) Ninety per cent of the differences in price from one sample to the next can be explained by corresponding differences in taste.

Answer(s) ☐   **(6 marks)**

? Question 18

Calculate the present value of an annuity of £2,800 per annum, payable at the end of each year for 10 years at a discount rate of 4 per cent. Use tables and give your answer to the nearest £.

Answer ☐   **(2 marks)**

? Question 19

An asset originally worth £80,000 depreciates at 28 per cent per annum. Find its value to the nearest £ at the end of 3 years.

Answer ☐   **(2 marks)**

? Question 20

If the following data are to be illustrated by means of a histogram and if the standard interval is taken to be 5 seconds, calculate the heights of the bars of the histogram (to the nearest whole number).

Time taken (seconds)	Frequency	Height of bar
0–5	47	☐
5–10	62	☐
10–20	104	☐
20–40	96	☐

(4 marks)

? Question 21

In an additive time series model, at a certain point of time, the actual value is 32,000 while the trend is 26,000 and the seasonal component is 6,200. If there is no cyclical variation, calculate the residual variation.

Answer ☐   **(2 marks)**

? Question 22

Solve the equation $2 \times x^2 - 5x - 7 = 0$ giving your answers correct to 1 d.p.

Answer ☐   **(2 marks)**

? Question 23

A project may result in the following profits with the probabilities stated.

Profit	Probability
£40,000	0.2
£25,000	0.4
(£12,000)	0.4

Calculate the expected profit to the nearest £.

Answer ☐   **(2 marks)**

? Question 24

If weights are normally distributed with mean 43 kg and standard deviation 6 kg, what is the probability of a weight being less than 50 kg?

Answer ☐   **(2 marks)**

? Question 25

A sum of £30,000 is invested at a nominal rate of 12 per cent per annum. Find its value after 3 years if interest is compounded every month. Give your answer to the nearest £.

Answer ☐   **(2 marks)**

? Question 26

Which one of the following is a disadvantage of using postal questionnaires as a method of contact with respondents in a survey?

(A) It omits the poorer sections of the population
(B) It is very expensive
(C) It gets very poor response rates
(D) It is subject to interviewer bias.

Answer ☐   **(2 marks)**

? Question 27

If $\Sigma x = 400$, $\Sigma y = 300$, $\Sigma x^2 = 18,000$, $\Sigma y^2 = 10,000$, $\Sigma xy = 13,000$ and $n = 10$,

(A) Calculate the value of 'b' in the regression equation, to 1 d.p.
(B) If the value of b were 0.9, calculate the value of 'a' in the regression equation to 1 d.p.

Answers
A ☐
B ☐   **(4 marks)**

? Question 28

In a time series analysis, the trend Y is given by the regression equation $Y = 462 + 0.34t$ where t denotes the quarters of years with 1st quarter of 2000 as $t = 1$.

(A) Predict the trend for the first quarter of 2004 to one d.p.

Answer ☐

(B) If the average seasonal variations are as follow

Quarter	Q1	Q2	Q3	Q4
Variation	−20%	0	−20%	+40%

Use the multiplicative model to predict the actual value for a 3rd quarter in which the trend prediction is 500.

Answer ☐   **(4 marks)**

? Question 29

A sales representative calls on three separate, unrelated customers and the chance of making a sale at any one of them is 0.7. Find the probability that a sale is made on the third call only, to 3 d.p.

Answer ☐   **(2 marks)**

? Question 30

Rearrange the formula $V = P \times (1 + r)^n$ to make r the subject.

Answer ☐   **(2 marks)**

? Question 31

In November, unemployment in a region is 238,500. If the seasonal component using an additive time series model is − 82,000, find the seasonally adjusted level of unemployment to the nearest whole number.

Answer ☐   **(2 marks)**

? Question 32

A company is planning capital investment for which the following year end cash flows have been estimated.

Year end	Net cash flow
Now	(10,000)
1	5,000
2	5,000
3	3,000

(A) Use tables to calculate the net present value (NPV) of the project using tables if the company has a cost of capital of 15 per cent.

Answer ☐

(B) If the NPV is £928 when the discount rate is 10 per cent and −£628 when it is 20 per cent, calculate the internal rate of return to two d.p.

Answer [_____]

(4 marks)

? Question 33

If the regression equation (in £'000) linking sales (Y) to advertising expenditure (X) is given by $Y = 4{,}000 + 12X$, forecast the sales when £150,000 is spent on advertising, to the nearest £.

Answer [_____]

(2 marks)

? Question 34

An item sells for £4.39 including value added tax at 17.5 per cent. If tax were reduced to 16 per cent, the new selling price to the nearest penny will be

(A) £4.33
(B) £4.01
(C) £4.32
(D) £5.09

Answer [_____]

(2 marks)

? Question 35

If $\Sigma f = 50$, $\Sigma fx = 120$ and $\Sigma fx^2 = 400$, calculate

(A) The mean (to 1 d.p.)
   Answer [_____]

(B) The standard deviation (to 1 d.p.)
   Answer [_____]

(4 marks)

? Question 36

The Economic Order Quantity (EOQ) for a particular stock item is given by the expression:

$$\text{EOQ} = \sqrt{\frac{2C_o D}{C_h}}$$

(A) If $C_o = £2$ per order, $D = 1{,}000$ items and $C_h = £0.25$ per item, then EOQ (rounded to the nearest whole number) will be

(A) 400
(B) 320
(C) 160
(D) 126

Answer [_____]

(B) If, for a different stock item, EOQ = 200 items, C_o = £4 per order and D = 1,000 items, then C_h (in £ per item) will be

(A) 0.05
(B) 0.10
(C) 0.15
(D) 0.20

Answer ☐ **(4 marks)**

? **Question 37**

A graphical presentation of classified data in which the number of items in each class is represented by the area of the bar is called

(A) an ogive.
(B) a histogram.
(C) a bar chart.
(D) a compound bar chart.

Answer ☐ **(2 marks)**

? **Question 38**

The following table shows the index of prices (1995 = 100) for a certain commodity over the period 1995–2000:

2000	2001	2002	2003	2004	2005
100	105	115	127	140	152

(A) The percentage increase in the price between 2000 and 2002 is nearest to

(A) 25.0
(B) 22.3
(C) 21.7
(D) none of these.

Answer ☐ **(2 marks)**

(B) It has been decided to rebase the index so that 2001 = 100. The index for 2003 will now be nearest to

(A) 193.1
(B) 139.4
(C) 125.0
(D) 119.7

Answer ☐ **(2 marks)**

? **Question 39**

The cost of an office desk is £263 plus value added tax of 17.5 per cent. Using the numbers given what Excel formula is required to calculate the total price to 2 d.p.?

Answer ☐ **(2 marks)**

Question 40

	A	B	C	D	E
1	IT Investment - Cash Out		250000		
2	Net IT Benefits	Year 1		66000	
3		Year 2		87000	
4		Year 3		98000	
5		Year 4		120000	
6		Year 5		110000	
7					
8	Fixed Cost of Capital or Interest Rate			24%	
9					
10	ROI				
11	NPV				
12					

Given the scenario in the spreadsheet above, what Excel formulae are required in

(A) Cell D10 to calculate the ROI
   Answer ☐

(B) Cell D11 to calculate the NPV
   Answer ☐   (4 marks)

Question 41

	A	B	C	D	E
1	INTEREST RATES AND CASH DEPOSITS				
2					
3	Interest rate	Deposit		Forecast	
4	10.00%	11550			
5	10.25%	11900			
6	10.50%	12500			
7	10.50%	11990			
8	10.75%	12900			
9	11.00%	13000			
10	11.25%	14000			
11	11.25%	13020			
12	11.25%	14000			
13	11.25%	14100			
14	11.50%	13380			
15	11.50%	14200			
16	11.75%	13500			
17	11.75%	14050			
18	12.00%	14500			
19	12.00%	14100			
20	12.25%	14500			
21	12.25%	14600			
22					

Given the scenario above, what Excel formula is required in cell D4 to calculate the forecast (using a least squared line approach)? Write your answer so that the formula can be copied into cells D5 through D21.
   Answer ☐   (2 marks)

? Question 42

	A	B	C	D	E	F	G
1			Average weight of pallets				
2	73	62	66	75	70	71	
3	83	69	74	79	78	82	
4	65	72	66	79	82	77	
5	69	61	63	80	82	66	
6	82	82	65	75	71	80	
7	74	84	72	78	67	84	
8							
9	Weight in kg.						
10	60						
11	65						
12	70						
13	75						
14	80						
15	85						
16							

Given the scenario above, what Excel formula is required in the range B10:B15 to calculate the frequency distribution of the pallet weights?

Answer ☐ (2 marks)

? Question 43

	A	B	C	D	E
1	Average daily temperature in degrees centigrade				
2	29	25	22	29	
3	24	26	25	28	
4	28	27	20	22	
5	21	20	24	24	
6	21	22	27	26	
7	23	26	21	24	
8	25	25	24	25	
9					
10	Median				
11	Mode				
12	Mean				
13					

Given the scenario above, what Excel formulae are required to calculate?

(A) The meadian (to 1 d.p.)
    Answer ☐

(B) The mode (to 0 d.p.)
    Answer ☐

(C) The mean (to 2 d.p.)
    Answer ☐ (3 marks)

? Question 44

Solve for y in the following inequalities.

(a) $-5x + 10y + 120 \geq 25x + 5y + 320$
    Answer ☐

(b) $240 + 8x \leq 12x + 10y + 140$
    Answer ☐ (2 marks)

? **Question 45**

(a) Describe the shaded area in the following Venn diagram.

    (A) Even numbers which begin with 3

    (B) Numbers that are even but do not have a 3 in them

    (C) The numbers 6, 12, 24, 30, 36

    (D) None of the above

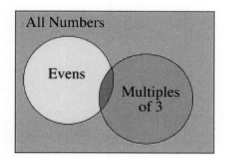

    Answer ☐

(b) If 50 people were asked whether they liked apples or oranges or both, 38 liked apples and 32 liked oranges. Use a Venn diagram to help you calculate how many people liked both?

    (A) 10

    (B) 15

    (C) 20

    (D) 25

                                                    (8 marks)

Mock Assessment – Solutions

✓ Solution 1

(A) 32 out of 250 items are faulty
Answer = 32/250 = 0.128

(B) 7 of the 53 items from P are faulty
Answer = 7/53 = 0.1321 (4 d.p.).

(C) 7 out of the 32 faulty items come from P
Answer = 7/32 = 0.2188 (4 d.p.).

✓ Solution 2

Total = 25 + 18 − 5 − 30 = 8
If we subtract 2 from each of the four averages they will add up to zero.

Answer: −30 − 2 = −32

✓ Solution 3

(B) describes a simple bar chart and (C) describes a compound or component bar chart. (D) is incorrect because a compound bar also shows several variables.

Answer: (A)

✓ Solution 4

$$r = [n\Sigma xy - \Sigma x \Sigma y]\big/\sqrt{\{[n\Sigma x^2 - (\Sigma x)^2] \times [n\Sigma y^2 - (\Sigma y)^2]\}}$$
$$= [10 \times 12{,}000 - 500 \times 200]/\sqrt{\{[10 \times 35{,}000 - 500^2][10 \times 9{,}000 - 200^2]\}}$$
$$= 20{,}000/\sqrt{\{100{,}000 \times 50{,}000\}} = 0.283 \,(3 \text{ d.p.})$$

Answer: 0.283

✓ Solution 5

Standard deviation uses all the data in a mathematically exact formula as a means of measuring variability. However, its one big disadvantage is that is greatly exaggerates the dispersion of skewed data so (C) is incorrect.

Answer: (C)

✓ Solution 6

15 year ratio = 250/12 = 20.83333
1 year ratio = $20.83333^{(1/15)}$ = 1.2244
Annual % increase = 22.4%

Answer: 22.4

✅ Solution 7

Events are independent if the occurrence of one does not alter the probability of the other, so (B) is correct. (A) and (C) are both definitions of mutually exclusive events.

Answer: (B)

✅ Solution 8

(A) Answer

Cf
5
25
80
98
100

(B) The upper quartile is at the three quarters point and its cf $= 100 \times 3/4 = 75$
   Answer: 75

✅ Solution 9

Seasonally adjusted value $=$ actual value/seasonal component. So seasonal component $=$ actual value divided by seasonally adjusted value $= 547/495 = 1.105$

Answer: 1.105

✅ Solution 10

Answer: (C)

that is, it is a stratified random sample.

✅ Solution 11

Value $= 15,000 \times 1.046^5 = £18,782$

Answer: 18,782

✅ Solution 12

(A) Wages are indexed with base 98 by dividing each year's wages figure by the '98 figure (i.e. by 426) and multiplying by 100.

Answers

97	98	99	00	01	02
97.2	100	103.3	105.6	109.9	112.7

(B) Value at '98 prices $= 116 \times 98$ RPI/'03 RPI $= 116 \times 172/204 = 97.8$
   Answer: 97.8

(C) An index of 96 means a drop of 4 per cent and, in this case, the drop is in the quantity of goods and services which the average wage buys. So the answer is (A).
Answer: (A)

✅ Solution 13

$(x^3)^2/x^4 = x^6/x^4 = x^{(6-4)} = x^2$

Answer: (D)

✅ Solution 14

$$\text{Maximum } Q/R = \text{Maximum } Q/\text{Minimum } R$$
$$= 34 \times 1.02/6.5 \times 0.96$$
$$= 5.558 \,(3 \text{ d.p.})$$

Answer: 5.558

✅ Solution 15

(A) Probability of failing is $1 - 0.48 = 0.52$
Probability of all three failing $= 0.52^3 = 0.1406$
Answer: 0.1406

(B) Probability of all three passing $= 0.48^3 = 0.1106$
Answer: 0.1106

✅ Solution 16

(A) There are 20 quarterly payments in 5 years, so the discount factor required is that corresponding to 3 per cent and 20 periods.
Answer: 14.878

(B) The method is to equate the present value of the repayments with the 100,000 borrowed. The cumulative discount factor at 3 per cent for 16 periods is 12.561 so $100,000 = 12.561X$

$X = 100,000/12.561 = £7,961$ (to the nearest £)
Answer: 7,961

(C) The present value of the saving scheme must be equated to that of £117,000 discounted at 2 per cent for 16 periods. The cumulative discount factor is 13.578 whilst the single discount factor is 0.728. Hence $13.578Y = 117,000 \times 0.728$ and $Y = £6,273$ (to nearest £).
Answer: 6,273

✅ Solution 17

(A) **Answer:** 8   5   6.5   6.5   4   3   1.5   1.5

(B) $R = 1 - 6\Sigma d^2/n(n^2 - 1) = 1 - 6 \times 150/8 \times 63 = -0.786$ (to 3 d.p.)
Answer: -0.786

(C) The value 0.9 means that there is a strong link between taste and price but it need not be linear. Because of the strange way in which taste is ranked, with the lowest rank being the best taste, rank of taste actually declines as price increases.
Answer: (d)

✓ Solution 18

The cumulative discount factor for 10 years at 4 per cent is 8.111, so the present value is $2,800 \times 8.111 = £22,711$ (to the nearest £)

Answer: 22,711

✓ Solution 19

If something declines at 28% per year, its value at the end of each year is only 72 per cent of its value at the start, so year-end value is start value times 0.72.
   Value after 3 years $= 80,000 \times 0.72^3 = £29,860$ (to the nearest £)

Answer: 29,860

✓ Solution 20

If the width of an interval is n times the standard width, then the height of its bar is frequency/n.
   Heights are 47, 62, 104/2 = 52 and 96/4 = 24.

Answers: 47, 62, 52, 24

✓ Solution 21

The formula for an additive time series is $A = T + S + R$ and hence residual $= A - T - S = 32,000 - 26,000 - 6,200 = -200$

Answer: -200

✓ Solution 22

Using the formula for the roots of a quadratic, $a = 2$, $b = -5$ and $c = -7$. Alternately, factorisation gives $(2x - 7)(x + 1) = 0$ and hence $x = -1$ or 3.5

Answers: -1, 3.5

✓ Solution 23

Expected profit (£'000) $= 40 \times 0.2 + 25 \times 0.4 - 12 \times 0.4 = 13.2$

Answer: 13,200

✅ Solution 24

$$P(W < 50) = P(z < [50 - 43]/6) = P(z < 1.17)$$
$$= 0.5 + \text{Normal table entry for } 1.17 = 0.5 + 0.3790$$
$$= 0.8790$$

Answer: 0.8790

✅ Solution 25

A nominal 12 per cent per annum means 1 per cent per month and in 3 years there are 36 months.
Value $= 30,000 \times 1.01^{36} = £42,923$ (to the nearest £).

Answer: 42,923

✅ Solution 26

Only (C) is a disadvantage of postal questionnaires. The other comments are not true.

Answer: (C)

✅ Solution 27

(A) $b = [n\Sigma xy - \Sigma x \Sigma y]/[n\Sigma x^2 - (\Sigma x)^2]$
$$= [10 \times 13,000 - 400 \times 300]/[10 \times 18,000 - 400^2] = 10,000/20,000$$
$$= 0.5$$
Answer: 0.5

(B) $A = \Sigma y/n - b \times \Sigma x/n = [300 - 0.9 \times 400]/10 = -6$
Answer: -6

✅ Solution 28

(A) For the 1st quarter of 2004, $t = 17$ and trend $Y = 462 + 0.34 \times 17 = 467.8$ (to 1 d.p.)
Answer: 467.8

(B) Prediction $=$ trend prediction reduced by $20\% = 500 \times 0.8$
Answer: 400

✅ Solution 29

$P(\text{not making a sale}) = 1 - P(\text{making a sale}) = 1 - 0.7 = 0.3$
$P(\text{sale at 3rd call only}) = P(\text{not at 1st}) \times P(\text{not at 2nd}) \times P(\text{sale at 3rd}) = 0.3 \times 0.3 \times 0.7 = 0.063$

Answer: 0.063

✅ Solution 30

$(1 + r)^n = V/P$ so $1 + r = (V/P)^{(1/n)}$ and $r = (V/P)^{(1/n)} - 1$

Answer: $(V/P)^{(1/n)} - 1$

✅ Solution 31

The additive model is $A = T + S$ and seasonal adjustment provides an estimate of $T = A - S = 238,500 - (-82,000) = 238,500 + 82,000$

Answer: 320,500

✅ Solution 32

(A)

Year	Cash flow	Discount factor	Present value
0	(10,000)	1	(10,000)
1	5,000	0.87	4,350
2	5,000	0.756	3,780
3	3,000	0.658	1,974
			NPV = 104

Answer: 104

(B) The IRR is the rate at which NPV is zero. NPV drops by £928 + £628 = £1,556 as the percentage rises from 10 per cent to 20 per cent that is by 10 per cent points. The drop per point is therefore 1,556/10 = £155.6. Since it starts at £928, the NPV will reach zero after an increase in the rate of 928/155.6 = 5.96% points. This occurs when the rate = 10 + 5.96 = 15.96% (to 2 d.p.)

Answer: 15.96

✅ Solution 33

When £150,000 is spent on advertising, $X = 150$ and $Y = 4,000 + 12 \times 150 = 5,800$. Forecast sales = 5,800 (£'000).

Answer: £5,800,000

✅ Solution 34

Price with VAT at 17.5% = 1.175 × Price without VAT
So price without VAT = 4.39/1.175
Price with VAT at 16% = 1.16 × Price without VAT = 1.16 × 4.39/1.175= £4.33

Answer: (A)

✔️ Solution 35

(A) Mean $= \Sigma fx / \Sigma f = 120/50 = 2.4$

Answer: 2.4

(B) Standard deviation $= \sqrt{[\Sigma fx^2 / \Sigma f - (\Sigma fx / \Sigma f)^2]} = \sqrt{[400/50 - (120/50)^2]}$

$$= \sqrt{2.24} = 1.5 \text{ (to 1 d.p.)}$$

Answer: 1.5

✔️ Solution 36

(A) $\text{EOQ} = \dfrac{\sqrt{2 C_0 D}}{C_h}$

$C_0 = 2, D = 1,000, C_h = 0.25$

$\therefore \text{EOQ} = \sqrt{\dfrac{2 \times 2 \times 1000}{0.25}} = \sqrt{\dfrac{4000}{0.25}} = \sqrt{16000}$

$\therefore \text{EOQ} = 126.49 = 26$

Answer: (D)

(B) $\text{EOQ} = 200, \ C_0 = 4, D = 1000$

$\therefore 200 = \sqrt{\dfrac{2 \times 4 \times 1,000}{C_h}} = \sqrt{\dfrac{8,000}{C_h}}$

$\therefore 200^2 = \dfrac{8000}{C_h}$

$\therefore C_h = \dfrac{8000}{40000} = 0.20$

Answer: (D)

✔️ Solution 37

An ogive doesn't have bars. A bar chart looks similar to a histogram but in a bar chart the height of the bar represents the frequency. In a histogram this is only the case if the classes are of equal width. In general the area of the bar in a histogram represents class frequency.
Answer: (B)

✔️ Solution 38

(A) % increase between 2000 and 2002:

$$\left(\frac{140 - 115}{115} \right) \times 100 = \frac{25}{115} \times 100 = 21.74$$

Answer: (C)

(B) Rebased price

$$\frac{152}{127} \times 100 = 119.69$$

Answer: (D)

✓ Solution 39

Answer: = ROUND(263 × 1.175,2)

✓ Solution 40

(A) **Answer:** = AVERAGE(D2:D6)/C1
(B) **Answer:** = NPV(D8,D2:D6) − C1

✓ Solution 41

Answer: = FORECAST(A4,$B$4:$B$31,$A$4:$A$31)

✓ Solution 42

Answer: = FREQUENCY(A2:F7,A10:A14)

✓ Solution 43

(A) **Answer:** = ROUND(MEDIAN(A2:D8),1)
(B) **Answer:** = ROUND(MODE(A2:D8),0)
(C) **Answer:** = ROUND(AVERAGE(A2:D8),2)

✓ Solution 44

(A) $10y - 5y \geq 25x + 5x + 200$
$5y \geq 30x+200$
$Y \geq 6 + 40$
(B) $-10y \leq 12x - 8x + 140 - 240$
$-10y \leq 4x - 100$
$-y \leq 0.4x - 10$
$Y \geq -0.4 + 10$

✓ Solution 45

(A) **Answer:** (D)
(B) **Answer:** (C)

Mock Assessment

Paper CO3
Fundamentals of Business Mathematics

? Question 1

£1,000 is to be shared between Christopher, Martin and Cameron in the ratio 24:22:14. How much does Martin receive?

(A) £265.54
(B) £325.68
(C) £366.66
(D) £421.25

? Question 2

If a good is priced at £745, including a sales tax of 17.5%, what is the price of the product excluding tax?

(A) £620.38
(B) £634.04
(C) £661.17
(D) £685.42

? Question 3

A table has five rows showing exam results and three columns showing schools in a town. Which of the following charts could be used to show the data?

 (i)   A single pie chart
 (ii) A multiple bar chart
(iii) A simple bar chart
(iv)   A component bar chart

(A) (i) and (ii)
(B) (ii) and (iii)
(C) (i) and (iv)
(D) (ii) and (iv)

? Questions 4 and 5 are based on the following data

The exam results for seven students were:

50, 55, 43, 52, 43, 62, 43.

❓ **Question 4**

The value of the mode is:

(A) 43
(B) 50
(C) 52
(D) 55

❓ **Question 5**

The median of the exam marks is:

(A) 43
(B) 50
(C) 52
(D) 55

❓ **Question 6**

What is the simplest way to express $2a^2 \times 3a^3$?

(A) $5a^5$
(B) $5a^6$
(C) $6a^5$
(D) $6a^6$

❓ **Question 7**

If $a = 2$ and $b = 4$, $x = 6$ and $y = 10$, then $\frac{a}{x} + \frac{b}{y}$ is equal to:

(A) $\dfrac{8}{10}$

(B) $\dfrac{13}{60}$

(C) $\dfrac{14}{15}$

(D) $\dfrac{15}{16}$

❓ **Questions 8 and 9 are based on the following data**

A bookshop sells a book for £24, which they buy in for £15.

❓ **Question 8**

The gross profit is:

(A) 25%
(B) 40%
(C) 50%
(D) 60%

? **Question 9**

The profit mark-up is:

(A) 50%
(B) 60%
(C) 66.66%
(D) None of the above

? **Question 10**

A student obtained 68% in a piece of coursework, 50% in his first exam and 48% in the final exam. The weightings were 20% coursework, 30% for exam 1 and 50% in the final exam. His result for the course was:

(A) 48%
(B) 50%
(C) 52.6%
(D) 55.4%

? **Question 11**

The difference between a biased and an unbiased error is:

(A) A biased error arises when individual items are rounded in the same direction and an unbiased error arises when individual items are rounded in either direction.
(B) A biased error arises when the individual items are not rounded.
(C) An unbiased error arises when the individual items are not rounded.
(D) None of the above.

? **Question 12**

A product has been reduced in price from £105.28 to £94.11. To two decimal places, the percentage reduction in price was:

(A) 11%
(B) 11.6%
(C) 11.61%
(D) 11.62%

? **Question 13**

If fixed cost is £5,000 and variable cost is equal to £100, then the formula for total cost may be written as:

(A) $100 + 5,000x$
(B) $100 + 5,100x$
(C) $£5,000 + 5,100x$
(D) $£5,000 + 100x$

？ Question 14

If $6x + 8y = 50$ and $20x + 4y = 76$, then the values of x and y are:

(A) $x = 3$: $y = 4$
(B) $x = 4$: $y = 5$
(C) $x = 6$: $y = 4$
(D) $x = 5$: $y = 6$

？ Questions 15 and 16 are based on the following information

A pack of cards consists of 52 playing cards divided into four suits of 13; hearts, diamonds, clubs and spades.

？ Question 15

What is the probability that a card selected at random is the queen of hearts?

(A) 1 in 52
(B) 1 in 26
(C) 1 in 13
(D) 1 in 4

？ Question 16

What is the probability of choosing three cards from the same suit in succession, assuming that once a card is picked it is not returned to the pack?

(A) 1%
(B) 3%
(C) 5%
(D) 7%

？ Question 17

The difference between a decision point and a random outcome point is:

(A) A decision point is where the decision maker has a choice. A random outcome point is outside the control of the decision maker.
(B) A random outcome is where the decision maker can make a choice. A decision point is outside the control of the decision maker.
(C) A decision point and a random outcome are similar statistical devices.
(D) A random outcome is a way of applying expected value criterion to situations where a number of decisions are made sequentially.

？ Question 18

A school is having a prize draw offering a £500 holiday to the winner. The tickets are on sale for 50p. If the £500 holiday was given to the school by a local travel company for £300, how many tickets would they need to sell to make a profit of £250. There are no other expenses.

(A) 950
(B) 1,000
(C) 1,050
(D) 1,100

❓ Question 19

If the population is known and a sample size of a certain number is required, then one in so many items is selected. This is known as:

(A) Random sampling
(B) Systematic sampling
(C) Cluster sampling
(D) Quota sampling

❓ Question 20

Which of the following is not a bar chart?

(A) Simple
(B) Component
(C) Multiple
(D) Pie

❓ Question 21

The upper quartiles show the value of:

(A) 25% through the cumulative frequencies
(B) 50% through the cumulative frequencies
(C) 75% through the cumulative frequencies
(D) 100% through the cumulative frequencies

❓ Question 22

The second decile represents the values of:

(A) 2% through the cumulative frequencies
(B) 20% through the cumulative frequencies
(C) 2% below the average
(D) 20% above the average

❓ Question 23

In a pie chart, if wages are represented by 60° and the total cost is £720,000, the amount paid out in wages is:

(A) £60,000
(B) £120,000
(C) £150,000
(D) £180,000

? Question 24

Which of the following is not an advantage of using the mean?

(A) It is easy to calculate
(B) All the data in the distribution is used
(C) It can be used in more advanced mathematical statistics
(D) It is not affected by extreme values

? Question 25

If the standard deviation is 1.2 and the arithmetic mean is 3.6, then the coefficient of variation is:

(A) 3
(B) 33.33
(C) 66.66
(D) 99.99

? Question 26

The standard deviation of 3, 5, 7, 8, 9, 11 is:

(A) 2.2
(B) 2.4
(C) 2.6
(D) 3.0

? Question 27

A normal distribution has a mean of 150 and a standard deviation of 20. 70% of this distribution is below:

(A) 155.4
(B) 158.3
(C) 160.6
(D) 172.5

? Question 28

In a normal distribution with a mean of 100, 7% of the population is above 120. The standard deviation of the distribution is:

(A) 10
(B) 13.33
(C) 16.67
(D) 20

? Questions 29–32 are based on the following information

A sample of light bulbs were found to have a mean life of 240 hours, with a standard deviation of 20 hours.

? Question 29

The standard error of the mean was:

(A) 1.29
(B) 2.29
(C) 3.29
(D) 4.29

? Question 30

The 95% confidence interval was between:

(A) 195.6 and 293.6
(B) 222.5 and 256.1
(C) 220 and 260
(D) 200.8 and 279.2

? Question 31

The 99% confidence interval level was between:

(A) 205 and 275
(B) 200 and 280
(C) 188.4 and 291.6
(D) 190 and 290

? Question 32

A sample standard deviation tends to underestimate the population standard deviation. A better estimate is known as:

(A) Bessel's correction
(B) Pearson's coefficient
(C) Point estimate of the parameter
(D) The Capie equivalent

? Question 33

In a forecasting model based on $Y = a$ and bx, the intercept is £750. If the value of $Y = £495$ and $x = 25$, then b is equal to:

(A) 12.25
(B) 15
(C) 17.50
(D) 25.75

? **Question 34**

The coefficient of determination $(R)2$ explains the:

(A) Percentage variation in the dependent variable, which is explained by the independent variable
(B) The relationship between the two variables
(C) The gradient, the intercept and the coefficient
(D) None of the above

? **Question 35**

A new vehicle costs £20,000. It is depreciated by 25% per annum on a reducing balance. At the end of year 3, the book value will be:

(A) £11,250.75
(B) £9,750.25
(C) £8,750.50
(D) £8,437.50

? **Question 36**

How much needs to be invested now at 5% to yield an annual income of £8,000 in perpetuity?

(A) £12,000
(B) £140,000
(C) £160,000
(D) £200,000

? **Question 37**

A landlord receives a rent of £1,000 to be received over ten successive years. The first payment is due now. If interest rates are 8%, then the present value of this income is equal to:

(A) £6,951
(B) £7,345
(C) £7,247
(D) £8,138

? **Question 38**

What is the annual repayment on a bank loan of £100,000 over 10 years at 7%?

(A) £13,141
(B) £14,236
(C) £15,123
(D) £16,981

? **Questions 39 and 40 are based on the following data**

In a time series, the multiplicative model is used to forecast sales and the following seasonal variations apply:

Quarter	1	2	3	4
Seasonal variation	1.2	1.8	0.6	?

The actual sales for the first two quarters of 2008 were:

Quarter 1	£110,000
Quarter 2	£125,000

? **Question 39**

The seasonal variation to the fourth quarter is:

(A) 0.2
(B) 0.4
(C) 0.6
(D) 0.8

? **Question 40**

The trend line for sales:

(A) Decreased between quarter 1 and quarter 2
(B) Increased between quarter 1 and quarter 2
(C) Remained constant between quarter 1 and quarter 2
(D) Cannot be determined from the information given

? **Question 41**

	A	B	C	D	E
1					
2	Amount invested	258000			
3	Cash flow year 1	73000			
4	Cash flow year 2	32000			
5	Cash flow year 3	27000			
6	Cash flow year 4	12000			
7					
8	Fixed cost of capital	15%			
9					
10					
11					

Given the above data, which of the following Excel functions and formula will calculate the ROI of the investment?

(A)   =ROI(B3:B6)/B2
(B)   =AVERAGE(B3:B6)–B2
(C)   =AVERAGE(B3:B6)/B2
(D)   =ROI(B3:B6)/B2*B8

(2 marks)

? **Question 42**

To find the mean of a number of values in a range labelled with the name OBSERVA-TIONS in an Excel spreadsheet, the following command should be entered into the required cell:

(A)   = MEDIAN(OBSERVATIONS)
(B)   = MEAN(OBSERVATIONS)
(C)   = MODE(OBSERVATIONS)
(D)   = AVERAGE(OBSERVATIONS)

(2 marks)

? **Question 43**

How would the calculation of the 6th root of 98 be entered into a spreadsheet?

(A) $=98^\wedge 1/6$
(B) $=98^\wedge (1/6)$
(C) $=1/6^\wedge 98$
(D) $=(1/6)^\wedge 98$

? **Question 44**

In the Excel spreadsheet below, cell B6 is called the:

(A)   work cell
(B)   current cell
(C)   active cell
(D)   key cell

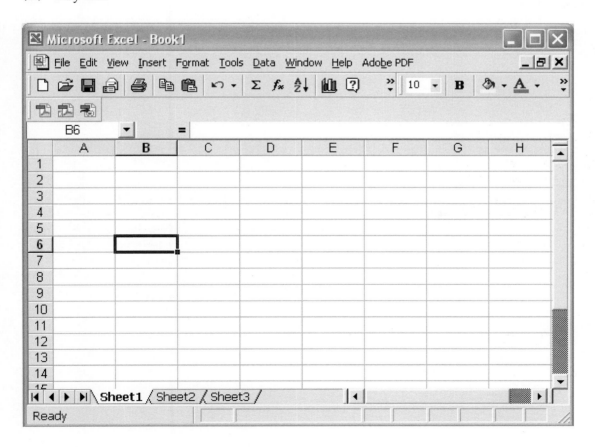

? **Question 45**

The following function has been typed into a cell within an Excel spreadsheet:

=IF(D6<>D7,"error","OK")

This is an example of:

(A) an error message
(B) a protected cell
(C) what–if analysis
(D) a control check

Mock Assessment – Solutions

✓ Solution 1

$24 + 22 + 14 = 60$

$\dfrac{22}{60} \times £1{,}000 = 366.66$

So C.

✓ Solution 2

$\dfrac{£745}{1.175} = £634.04$

So B.

✓ Solution 3

A simple bar chart and a simple pie chart could not hold this amount of information.

So D – (ii) and (iv).

✓ Solution 4

The mode is the value which appears the most frequently, so 43 appears 3 times.

So A.

✓ Solution 5

The median is the value of the middle item in a distribution. There are 3 marks above 50 and 3 marks below, so 50 is mode.

So B.

✓ Solution 6

We need to multiply the numbers and add the powers, so $2a^2 \times 3a^3$ becomes $6a^5$.

So C.

✓ Solution 7

$$\dfrac{2}{6} + \dfrac{6}{10} = \dfrac{10}{30} + \dfrac{18}{30}$$

$$= \dfrac{28}{30} = \dfrac{14}{15}$$

So C.

✓ Solution 8

Gross profit is % of sales

So $\dfrac{10}{25} = 40\%$

So B.

✓ Solution 9

The profit mark-up is the % mark-up on cost

So $\dfrac{10}{15} = 66.66\%$

So C.

✓ Solution 10

$0.2 \times 68 + 0.3 \times 50 + 0.5 \times 48$

$$
\begin{array}{r}
13.6 \\
15.0 \\
\underline{24.0} \\
\underline{52.6}
\end{array}
$$

✓ Solution 11

Answer A.

✓ Solution 12

$$
\begin{array}{r}
£105.28 \\
\underline{£94.11} \\
\underline{£11.17}
\end{array}
$$

Answer is 10.61, so C.

✓ Solution 13

$£5,000 + 100x$

Total cost is fixed cost plus variable cost. Fixed cost remains at the same level regardless of output.

So D.

✓ Solution 14

$$6x + 8y = 50$$
$$20x + 4y = 76$$

Multiply equation 2 by 2

$6x + 8y = 50$
$40x + 8y = 152$

Subtracting equation 1 from 2

$34x \quad = 102$
$\quad x \quad = 3$
$6x + 8y = 50$
$6x \quad = 18$
$\quad\quad 8y = 32$
$\quad\quad y = 4$
$x = 3y = 4$

So A.

✅ Solution 15

There are 4 queens, there are 13 hearts but only 1 queen of hearts, so 1 in 52.

Answer A.

✅ Solution 16

The first card picked could be from any suit but there will be only 12 left of that suit from 51 when we draw the second card, and 11 from 50 when we draw the third, so:

$$\frac{12}{51} \times \frac{11}{50} \quad \frac{132}{2550}$$

Answer 0.05.

So 5% – C.

✅ Solution 17

Answer A.

✅ Solution 18

Cost to the school – £300.

To cover costs, we would need to sell 600 × 50p, and to make a £250 profit we would need to sell 500 × 50p, so 1100.

So D.

✅ Solution 19

This is known as systematic sampling.

So B.

✓ Solution 20

A pie chart is a circle.

So D.

✓ Solution 21

75% through the cumulative frequencies.

So C.

✓ Solution 22

20% through the cumulative frequencies.

So B.

✓ Solution 23

There are $360°$ in a circle, so if wages represent $60°$, that is $\frac{1}{6}$ of total cost:

$$\frac{1}{6} \times £720,000 = £120,000$$

So B.

✓ Solution 24

The mean is affected by extreme values, e.g. if nine people earn £100 per week, and one person earns £1,100, that makes the mean wage £200 when 90% of the sample earn half of the mean.

So D.

✓ Solution 25

Coefficient of variation

$$= \frac{\text{standard deviation} \times 100}{\text{arithmetic mean}}$$

so $\dfrac{120}{3.6} = 33.33$

So B.

✓ Solution 26

x	x^2
3	9
5	25
7	49
8	64
9	81
11	121
$\Sigma 43$	$\Sigma x^2\ 349$

$$\Pi = \sqrt{\frac{349}{6} - \frac{43^2}{6^2}}$$
$$= \sqrt{58.16 - 51.36}$$
$$= \sqrt{6.8}$$
$$= 2.6$$

So C.

✅ Solution 27

From the normal distribution table, 20% of a distribution table lies between the mean and 0.53 standard deviation above the mean:

so $\quad x = 150 \times (0.53 \times 20)$
$\qquad = 160.6$

So C.

✅ Solution 28

If 7% of the population is above 120, then $0.5 - 0.07 = 0.43$.

so $\qquad 2 = 1.5$
$\qquad 1.5 = 120 - 100$

$$v = \frac{20}{1.5} = 13.33$$

So B.

✅ Solution 29

$$\text{Standard error} = \frac{\delta}{\sqrt{n}} = \frac{20}{\sqrt{240}} = 1.29$$

So A.

✅ Solution 30

$240 \pm (20 \times 1.96)$
$240 + 39.2 = 279.2$
$240 - 39.2 = 200.8$

We can be 95% confident that bulbs will last between 200.8 hours and 279.2 hours.

So. D.

✓ Solution 31

$$240 \pm (20 \times 2.58)$$
$$= 240 + 51.6 = 291.6$$
$$= 240 - 51.6 = 188.4$$

So C.

✓ Solution 32

Answer A.

✓ Solution 33

$$495 = 250 + 25b$$

$$\frac{495 - 250}{20} = \frac{245}{20} = 12.25$$

So A.

✓ Solution 34

Answer A.

✓ Solution 35

Year 1	Depreciation	5,000
	Book value	15,000
Year 2	Depreciation	3,750
	Book value	11,250
Year 3	Depreciation	2,812.50
	Book value	8,437.50

So D.

✓ Solution 36

$$£8,000 \times \frac{1}{0.05} = £160,000$$

So C.

✓ Solution 37

NPV = £1,000 (1 + 6.247)

See cumulative present value table:

$$= £1,000 \times 7.247$$
$$= £7,247$$

So C.

☑ Solution 38

Present value of 10 repayments of x at 7% = £100,000

From table $x = \dfrac{£100,000}{7.024}$

$\qquad\quad = 14{,}236$

So B.

☑ Solution 39

This is a multiplicative model, so seasonal variations should sum to 4, with an average of 1 if there are four quarters.

If Y is seasonal variation for Quarter 4:

$$1.2 + 1.8 + 0.6 = Y = 4$$
$$Y = 4 - 3.6$$
$$Y = 0.4$$

So B.

☑ Solution 40

	Quarter 1	Quarter 2
Seasonal component	1.2	1.8
Actual sales	110,000	125,000
Trend	91,666	69,444

Trend has decreased between Quarter 1 and Quarter 2.

So A.

☑ Solution 41

The answer is (C)

Working

Whilst Excel often does use the term you would expect in a function such as =NPV, at other times (such as with ROI) the word is less obvious.

☑ Solution 42

The answer is (D)

Working

Excel can also find the MEDIAN and the MODE by substituting those words in the command.

✓ Solution 43

The answer is (b)

Working

(A)   Is wrong because without the brackets around the 1/6, the calculation would be 98 to the power 1, divided by 6.
(B)   Is correct
(C)   Is wrong. This would calculate 1 divided by 6 to the power of 98
(D)   Is wrong. This would calculate 1/6 to the power of 98 (the same answer as c)

✓ Solution 44

The answer is (c)

✓ Solution 45

The answer is (d)

Working

The formula will alert the user if the two figures in cells D6 and D7 are not the same. If they are, the message will read 'OK', if not it will read 'error'. This may be used to check, for example, that the horizontal and vertical totals in a table are the same.